Letters from Readers of
What I Wish I Knew When I Was 20

"Your book left a huge impression on me. . . . Never have I read a book so intently from start to finish in one sitting."

—Windsor

"I must thank you for showing that nearly everything is attainable, as long as you trust yourself and use your brain and heart to deliver."

—Misha

"By the third page, I was hooked and wishing that I was a student in one of your classes at Stanford. . . . I feel more empowered and inspired than ever."

—Starry

"*What I Wish I Knew When I Was 20* was the most wonderful book I have ever read about self-improvements, motivations, and life lessons . . . a crash course that changed my life and the way I think."

—Angely

"This is simply a thank-you note. . . . *What I Wish I Knew When I Was 20* was figuratively a resuscitation to the right hemisphere of my brain."

—Amer

"Thank you for inspiring me to look beyond my screen of assumptions and recognize the world as being full of opportunity and promise merely waiting to be discovered."

—Sophia

"I loved the book . . . it made my weekend and now my life. It's a real inspiration."

—Soujanya

"Today, on my twentieth birthday, I happened upon your *What I Wish I Knew When I Was 20* book at the Stanford bookstore. I've already read half of it and am emailing to thank you. . . . Finding your book today was the best birthday gift I could have asked for. It was inspiring to read concrete examples of the concepts I've been trying to piece together."

—Nadia

"I have just finished reading *What I Wish I Knew When I Was 20* and just had to thank you so much. . . . You should also know it really made me think differently, it was so inspiring. Well, I hope you get the message just so you know you have a really huge fan down here in Argentina."

—Agustina

"I stumbled across your book just at the perfect time and it has had a great impact on the way I feel about the uncertainty of the next year ahead of me."

—Nisha

"This book provided the extra jolt I needed to keep moving forward."

—Cesar

"I took some of your lessons about innovation and applied them in a truly old-school firm. The results were nothing short of amazing! In one session, with similar tools to what you described in the first chapter of your book, we identified over $150 million in new opportunities!"

—Francisco

"I won't be twenty again and it's been a long time since I was, but after finishing your book, I felt the buzz of possibility that I wish I'd had at that age."

—Ben

"I picked up your book yesterday and could not put it down. I was hooked immediately. I recognized that the wisdom you shared in this book is crucial for the next steps I need to take in my own journey."

—Laurie

"I admit to being a confused college student lacking direction in life and harboring plenty of fear about graduating. Reading this book today was exactly what I needed. I think tomorrow I will read it again, this time armed with a highlighter and a pack of Post-Its."

—Catherine

"After reading it cover to cover, I felt at once reassured and inspired. I can't imagine a better book to have read right before heading off to college."

—Haley

"I finished your book *What I Wish I Knew When I Was 20* and have since bought up all the copies I could lay my hands on at bookstores. The copies have now been distributed to all my friends hoping to make an entrepreneurial move in life."

—Jennifer

Also by Tina Seelig

inGenius: A Crash Course on Creativity

*Creativity Rules: Get Ideas Out of Your Head
and Into the World*

What I Wish I Knew When I Was 20

A Crash Course on Making Your Place in the World

———— *10th Anniversary Edition* ————

TINA SEELIG

HarperOne
An Imprint of HarperCollins*Publishers*

For Josh,

Happy 10-Year Anniversary

of your 20th Birthday!

HarperOne

HarperCollins books may be purchased for educational, business, or sales promotional use. For information, please email the Special Markets Department at SPsales@harpercollins.com.

First HarperOne hardcover published in 2009
First HarperOne paperback published in 2010

Designed by Paula Russell Szafranski

Library of Congress Cataloging-in-Publication Data
has been applied for.

ISBN 978-0-06-294258-6

19 20 21 22 23   LSC   10 9 8 7 6 5 4 3 2

CONTENTS

Foreword   ix

1   Buy One, Get Two Free   1

2   The Upside-Down Circus   15

3   Bikini or Die   35

4   Please Take Out Your Wallets   53

5   The Secret Sauce of Silicon Valley   69

6   Turbulence Ahead   81

7   No Way . . . Engineering Is for Girls   97

8   Turn Lemonade into Helicopters   113

9   Are You Smart or Right?   137

10 Paint the Target Around the Arrow   153

11 Will This Be on the Exam?   163

12 Experimental Artifacts   179

Author's Letter   195
Acknowledgments   199
Notes   203
Index   209

FOREWORD

Thank you so much for picking up this book. It is truly an honor to be able to share the updated edition of *What I Wish I Knew When I Was 20* with you.

The original book came out in the Spring of 2009, the week of my son Josh's twentieth birthday. As we approached the ten-year anniversary of the book, I read it through again. It was a treat to experience the words with fresh eyes and fascinating to see which concepts and stories stood the test of time. Most had; some were dated. And with ten years of additional experience, I knew more than I did when I wrote the first edition. Therefore, I asked my publisher if I could write a ten-year anniversary edition of the book. To my delight, they said yes!

This edition has a structure similar to the original, with many new examples drawn both from my classroom and from innovators operating in different settings. Additionally, I have included many new insights gained over the last decade. There are two additional chapters to accommodate all of the new material.

Overall, my objective as an educator and in this book is to be a provocateur—to ask questions, tell stories, and set up scenarios that lead to surprising insights. In my classroom, my hope is that every student is changed by each experience, feeling more empowered by the exercises and concepts that are presented. The goal of this book is the same. I hope that after reading it you will have an enlarged set of tools for seeing and seizing the opportunities around you.

This edition will come out on Josh's thirtieth birthday. I'm forever grateful to him for inspiring me to write. I'm also very appreciative of the students and colleagues with whom I've had the privilege to learn over the years.

Please feel free to reach out to me with your reactions. I welcome feedback and look forward to hearing which parts of the book are most meaningful to you. I can be reached at tseelig@gmail.com or via my website at tinaseelig.com. You can also follow me on Twitter @tseelig.

Chapter 1

Buy One, Get Two Free

What would you do to earn money if all you had was five dollars and two hours? This is the assignment I gave students in my very first course at the Stanford d.school.[1] The rules were simple: each of fourteen teams received an envelope with five dollars of "seed funding" and was told they could spend as much time as they wanted planning. However, once they cracked open the envelope, they had two hours to generate as much money as possible. I gave them from Wednesday afternoon until Sunday evening to complete the assignment. Then, on Sunday evening, each team had to send me one slide describing what they had done, and on Monday afternoon each team had three minutes to present their project to the class. They were encouraged to be entrepreneurial by identifying opportunities, challenging assumptions, leveraging the limited resources they had, and being creative.

What would you do if you were given this challenge? When I ask this question to most groups, someone usually shouts out "Go to Las Vegas" or "Buy a lottery ticket." This gets a big laugh. These folks would take a significant risk in return for a small chance of earning a big reward. The next most common suggestion is to set up a car wash or lemonade stand, using the five dollars to purchase starting materials. This is a fine option for anyone interested in earning a few extra dollars of spending money in two hours. But most of the students eventually found a way to move far beyond the standard responses. They took seriously the challenge to question traditional assumptions, exposing a wealth of possibilities, in order to create as much value as possible.

How did they do this? Here's a clue: the teams that made the most money didn't use the five dollars at all. They realized that focusing on the money actually framed the problem way too tightly. They understood that five dollars is nearly nothing and decided to reinterpret the problem more broadly: What can you do to make money if you start with *nothing*?

They ramped up their observation skills, tapped into their talents, and unlocked their creativity to identify problems in their midst—problems they experienced or noticed others experiencing, problems they might have seen before but had never thought to solve. These problems were nagging but not necessarily at the forefront of anyone's mind. By unearthing these problems and then working to solve them, the winning team brought in more than six hundred dollars, and the average return on the five-dollar investment was 4,000 percent! If you take into account that many of the teams didn't use the funds at all, then their financial returns were infinite.

So, *what did they do?*

One group identified a problem common in a lot of college towns—the frustratingly long lines at popular restaurants on Saturday nights. The team decided to help those people who didn't want to wait in line. They paired off and booked reservations at several restaurants. As the times for their reservations approached, they sold each reservation for up to twenty dollars to customers who were happy to avoid a long wait.[2]

As the evening wore on, the students made several interesting observations. First, they realized that the female students were better at selling the reservations than the male students, probably because customers were more comfortable being approached by the young women. They adjusted their plan so that the male students ran around town making reservations at different restaurants while the female students sold those places in line. They also learned that the entire operation worked best at restaurants that use vibrating pagers to alert customers when their table is ready. Physically swapping pagers with those who received one later made customers feel as though they were receiving something tangible for their money. They were more comfortable handing over their money and pager in exchange for the new pager. This had an additional bonus—teams could then sell the newly acquired pager as the later reservation time grew nearer.

Another team took an even simpler approach. They set up a stand in front of the student union where they offered to measure bicycle tire pressure for free. If the tires needed filling, they added air for one dollar. At first they thought they were taking advantage of their fellow students, who could easily go to a nearby gas station to have their tires filled. But after their first few customers, the students realized the bicyclists were incredibly grateful. Even though the cyclists could get their tires filled for free nearby, and the task was easy for the students to perform, the students were providing a convenient and valuable service. In fact, halfway through the two-hour period, the team stopped asking for a specific payment and requested donations instead. Their income soared! They made much more when their customers were reciprocating for a free service than when asked to pay a fixed price. For this team, as well as for the team making restaurant reservations, experimenting along the way paid off. The iterative process, in which small changes are made in response to customer feedback, allowed them to optimize their strategy on the fly.

Each of these projects brought in a few hundred dollars, and their fellow classmates were duly impressed. However, the team that generated the greatest profit looked at the resources at their disposal through a completely different lens, and made $650. These students determined that the most valuable asset they had was neither the five dollars nor the two hours. Instead, their insight was that their most precious resource was their three-minute presentation time in class. They decided to sell it to a company that wanted to recruit students in the class. The team created a three-minute commercial for that company and showed it to the students during their presentation time. This was brilliant! They recognized they had a fabulously valuable asset—creative students who were looking for jobs—just waiting to be mined.

Each of the other eleven teams found clever ways to earn money, including running a photo booth at the annual Viennese Ball, selling maps that highlighted local restaurants during Parents' Weekend, and designing and selling a custom T-shirt to the students in the class. One team actually lost money when the students purchased umbrellas to sell in San Francisco on a rainy day, only to have the weather clear up shortly after they launched their effort. And, yes, one team ran a car wash and another started a lemonade stand, but their returns were much lower than average.

I count the Five-Dollar Challenge as a success in teaching students about having an entrepreneurial mindset. But it left me feeling a bit uncomfortable. I didn't want to communicate that value is always measured in terms of financial rewards. So, I added a twist the next time I assigned the project. Instead of five dollars, I gave each team an envelope containing ten paper clips. Teams were told they had four hours over the next few days to generate as much "value" as possible using the paper clips, and value could be measured in *any way they wanted*.

The inspiration for this was the story of Kyle MacDonald, who started with one red paper clip and traded up until he had a house![3] He set up a blog to document his progress and to solicit trades. It took a year, but step-by-step he reached his goal. He traded the red paper clip for a fish-shaped pen. He then traded the pen for a doorknob and the doorknob for a Coleman stove, and so on. The value of the items increased slowly but surely over the year until he had his dream house! Considering what Kyle did with *one* paper clip, I felt quite generous giving the students *ten* paper clips. The assignment began on a Thursday morning, and presentations were scheduled for the following Tuesday.

By the time Saturday rolled around, however, I was anxious. Perhaps I'd gone too far this time. I worried the assignment would be a bust and was ready to chalk it up to experience. These concerns couldn't have been further from the mark. The seven student teams each chose to measure "value" in different ways. One decided that paper clips were the new currency and went about collecting as many as possible. Another team learned that the current world record for the longest paper-clip chain was more than twenty-two miles and set out to break that record. They rallied their friends and roommates, pitched local stores and businesses on their plan, and showed up in class with a mountain of paper clips linked together. Apparently, the students in their dorm were so moved by the challenge that they committed themselves to breaking the world record even after the assignment was over. (I'm pretty sure they didn't break the record, but it's a good measure of the energy the team was able to generate.)

The most entertaining and provocative team came to class with a short video, with the song "Bad Boys" blaring in the background, that showed them using the paper clips to pick locks and break into dorm rooms to steal tens of thousands of dollars' worth of sunglasses, cell phones, and computers. Just before I fainted, they announced that they were joking and showed another video documenting what they really had done. They traded the paper clips for some poster board and set up a stand at a nearby shopping center with a sign that read, STANFORD STUDENTS FOR SALE: BUY ONE, GET TWO FREE. They were surprised by the offers they received. They started out carrying heavy bags for shoppers, moved on to taking out the recycling from a clothing store, and eventually did an ad hoc brainstorming session for a woman who needed help solving a business problem. She paid them with three older computer monitors she didn't need.

Over the years, I've continued to give groups similar assignments, changing the starting material from paper clips to Post-it notes, rubber bands, water bottles, and unmatched socks. In fact, I never give the same challenge twice, since I don't want to be anchored by prior solutions. Each time the students surprise me, and themselves, by what they accomplish with limited time and resources. For example, using one small package of Post-it notes, students created a collaborative music project, a campaign to educate people about heart disease, and a public service commercial—called "Unplug-It"—about saving energy.

This exercise ultimately evolved into what became known as the Innovation Tournament, with hundreds of teams from all over the world participating.[4] Participants use the competition as a means to look at the world around them with fresh eyes, identifying opportunities in their own backyard. They challenge traditional assumptions and, in doing so, generate enormous value from practically nothing. The entire adventure with Post-it notes was captured on film and became the foundation for a professional documentary called *Imagine It!*[5]

These exercises highlight several counterintuitive points. First, opportunities are abundant. At any place and time you can look around and identify problems that need solving. Some are mundane, such as scoring a table at a popular restaurant or pumping up bike tires. Many are much larger, relating to major world issues. The lesson is that most problems are opportunities, and the bigger the problem, the bigger the opportunity.[6]

Second, most people approach problems as though they can't be solved and, therefore, don't see the creative solutions sitting right in front of them. However, regardless of the size of a problem, there are usually creative ways to use the resources already at your disposal to solve it. This is actually the definition my colleagues and I use for entrepreneurship: an entrepreneur is someone who is always on the lookout for problems that can be turned into opportunities and finds creative ways to leverage limited resources to reach their goals.

Third, we so often frame problems too tightly. When given a simple challenge, such as earning money in two hours, most people quickly jump to standard responses. They don't step back and look at the problem more broadly. Taking off the blinders and reframing the problem opens up a world of possibilities. Students who participated in these projects took this lesson to heart. Many reflected afterward that they would never have an excuse for being broke since there is always a nearby problem begging to be solved.

• • •

These assignments grew out of a course I teach on entrepreneurship and innovation at Stanford University. The overarching goal is to demonstrate that all problems can be viewed as opportunities for creative solutions. We first focus on individual creativity, then move on to creativity in teams, and finally dive into creativity and innovation in organizations. We start with small challenges and slowly make them more difficult. As the course progresses, the students grow increasingly comfortable seeing problems through the lens of possibility and are eventually willing to take on just about anything that comes their way.

I've been at Stanford for twenty years, codirecting the Stanford Technology Ventures Program (STVP),[7] which is located in the School of Engineering. STVP's mission is to teach scientists and engineers about entrepreneurship and to provide them with the tools they need to be entrepreneurial in whatever role they play. We believe, along with a growing number of universities around the world, that it isn't good enough for students to come out of school with a purely technical education. To be successful, they need to understand how to be entrepreneurial leaders in all working environments and in every part of their lives. As Tom Byers, my partner at STVP, first said, "Entrepreneurship is a Trojan horse for teaching a wide range of skills that are relevant in all settings."

STVP focuses on teaching, scholarly research, and outreach to students, faculty, and entrepreneurs around the world. We strive to create "T-shaped people," with a depth of knowledge in at least one discipline and a breadth of knowledge and skills that allows them to work effectively with professionals in other disciplines to bring their ideas to life. No matter what their role, having an entrepreneurial mindset is key to solving problems, from small challenges that face each of us every day to looming world crises that require the attention and efforts of the entire planet. In fact, entrepreneurship requires a range of skills, from leadership and team building to negotiation, innovation, and decision-making.

I'm also on the faculty of the Hasso Plattner Institute of Design at Stanford, affectionately called the d.school. This cross-disciplinary institute draws upon educators from across the entire university, including the Schools of Engineering, Medicine, Business, and Education. The institute was envisioned and launched by Stanford mechanical engineering professor David Kelley, who is also the founder of the design firm IDEO, known for creating wildly inventive products and experiences. All d.school courses are taught by at least two professors from different disciplines and cover an endless array of topics, from designing for extreme affordability to creating infectious action to designing for agile aging. As part of the d.school teaching team, I've experienced the thrill of radical collaboration, extreme brainstorming, and rapid prototyping as we give our students and ourselves big, messy problems with more than one right answer.

The stories in this book come out of our classrooms at Stanford, as well as from my prior experiences as a scientist, entrepreneur, management consultant, educator, and author. Other stories come from those who have taken a wide range of paths, including entrepreneurs, inventors, artists, and academics. I'm fortunate to be surrounded by people who have done remarkable things by challenging assumptions and who were eager to share their tales of success and failure.

Many of the ideas presented here are the polar opposite of the lessons we are taught in the traditional education system. In fact, the rules that apply in school are often completely different from those in the outside world. This disparity causes incredible stress when we leave school and attempt to find our own way. Gracefully bridging that gap to tackle real-world challenges can be extremely difficult, but it's doable with the right tools and mindset.

For example, in school, students are usually evaluated as individuals and graded on a curve. In short, when they win, someone else loses. Not only is this stressful, but it isn't how most organizations work. Outside school, people usually work in a team with a shared goal, and when they win, so does everyone else. In fact, in the business world there are usually small teams embedded inside larger teams, and at every level the goal is to make everyone successful.

The typical classroom has a teacher who views his or her job as pouring information into the students' brains. The door to the room is closed, and the chairs are bolted to the floor, facing the teacher. Students take careful notes, knowing they will be tested on the material later. For homework, they are asked to read assigned material from a textbook and quietly absorb it on their own. This couldn't be any more different from life after college, where people are their own teachers, charged with figuring out what they need to know, where to find the information, and how to absorb it. In fact, real life is the ultimate open-book exam. The doors are thrown wide open, allowing everyone to draw on endless resources around them as they tackle open-ended problems related to work, family, friends, and the world at large. Carlos Vignolo, a masterful professor at the University of Chile, told me that he provocatively suggests that students take classes from the worst teachers in their school because this will prepare them for life, in which they won't always have talented educators leading the way.

Additionally, in large classes, students are typically evaluated by multiple-choice tests, with one right answer for every question, and the bubbles must be carefully filled in with number-two pencils to make for easy grading. In sharp contrast, in most situations outside school there are a multitude of answers to every question, many of which are correct in some way.

Sadly, this happens around the world. I recently received a disturbing email from a young person from South Korea. Her teacher had marked her wrong on a multiple-choice test, and she wanted to contest the answer. So, she reached out to me for support.

What was the problem? Her teacher had assigned a passage from this very book. The reading was about seeing the potential in the craziest ideas. Students had to read the passage and answer a multiple-choice question to demonstrate they understood the paragraph. However, the question was written in such a way that even I couldn't answer it. It seemed to be designed to confuse the students, and it clearly didn't test whether they understood the meaning of the passage. I wrote back to the student with my thoughts on the test question, explaining that it was a trick question. It beautifully illustrated the concept that "not everything that can be counted counts, and not everything that counts can be counted."[8]

The world is filled with choices, and many things that matter deeply, such as love, ethics, and creativity, can't easily be counted. There isn't one right answer that leads to a clear reward. Although family, friends, and teachers will happily give us pointed advice about what to do, it is essentially our responsibility to pick our own direction. And we don't have to be right the first time. Life usually presents many opportunities to experiment and recombine our skills and passions in new and surprising ways.

Even more important, it should be acceptable to fail. In fact, failure is an important part of life's learning process. Just as evolution is a series of trial-and-error experiments, life is full of false starts and inevitable stumbling. Not one of us walked the first time we tried, or rode a bicycle on our first attempt. Why should we expect students and adults to complete complicated tasks on the first try? The key to success is the ability to extract the lessons out of every experience and to move on with that new knowledge.

The following chapters are designed to challenge you to see yourself and the world in a fresh light. The ideas are straight-forward, but not necessarily intuitive. As an educator focusing on innovation and entrepreneurship, I have seen firsthand that these ideas are relevant to individuals working in all dynamic environments, where situations change rapidly, requiring those involved to know how to identify opportunities, balance priori-ties, and learn from failure. Additionally, the concepts are valu-able to anyone who wants to squeeze the most juice out of life.

Essentially, I want to provide you with a new way to view the obstacles you encounter every day while charting your course into the future. In addition, I hope you will give yourself per-mission to question conventional wisdom and revisit the rules around you. There will always be uncertainty at each turn, but when you are armed with the confidence that comes from see-ing how others have coped with similar ambiguities, the stress in your life will morph into excitement, and the challenges you face will become opportunities.

Chapter 2

The Upside-Down Circus

Why don't most of us view problems as opportunities in our everyday lives? Why did the teams described in the prior chapter have to wait for a class assignment to stretch the limits of their imaginations? Essentially, we aren't taught to embrace problems. We're taught that problems are to be avoided, or something to complain about. In fact, while speaking at a conference for business executives, I presented video clips from the Innovation Tournament as part of my talk. Later that afternoon the CEO of a large company approached me and lamented that he wished he could go back to school, where he would be given open-ended problems and be challenged to be creative. I looked at him with confusion. I was pretty confident that every day he faced real-life challenges that would benefit from creative thinking. Unfortunately, he didn't see that the concepts easily related to his life and business. He viewed my assignments as something that could happen only in a controlled, academic environment. Of course, that isn't and shouldn't be the case.

We can and should challenge ourselves every single day. That is, we can choose to view the world through the lens of possibilities. The more we take on problems, the more confident and proficient we become at solving them. And the better able we are to see them as opportunities.

Here is a very personal example. Recently, I woke up super early to complete final preparations for a lecture I was scheduled to give that morning. It was dark at 5:30 a.m., and I could hardly see a thing. Trying to be as quiet as possible, I slid out of bed and made my way to the bedroom door . . . *Bang!* I smashed my toe.

The pain running through my body was just as palpable as my frustration. I had planned to do final prep work on my talk, and now I would be spending the time icing my toe. I hobbled downstairs to the kitchen and found a bag of frozen peas. While I tended to my toe, which was already turning a lovely shade of purple, my husband walked in. He turned to me and said, "Remember, every problem is an opportunity." Those words, which I frequently use, were *not* funny in this situation. Clearly, this was not an opportunity!

However, after a few minutes I started thinking, *Okay, how do I turn a smashed toe into an opportunity?* An idea came to me and took shape as I showered. I was going to find a way to weave this into my talk. So, here is what I said:

> I don't usually give lectures wearing my sneakers. But this morning I smashed my toe quite badly. Not only did this accident give me an excuse to wear more comfortable shoes, but it also encouraged me to think about the opportunity hidden in plain sight, namely

the many examples of thriving companies that grew out of painful disappointments. This is what entrepreneurs do! They see the possibilities where others see problems. Slack, the wildly successful messaging platform, grew out of a failing gaming company. Even though the game wasn't catching on, the integrated messaging tool it used was a hit. This was also the case with Instagram, which grew out of a failing web application. The founders, Kevin Systrom and Mike Krieger, threw out their initial product, Burbn, which was supposed to help friends connect, and poured all of their efforts into the photo-sharing feature inside the application. My smashed toe is a poignant reminder that we need to look at the potential presented by potholes.

Then I launched into my prepared talk about the importance of having an attitude that allows you to see and seize opportunities. It was amazing how much energy my opening story generated in the room, and in me. It created a hook I returned to throughout the lecture and helped build a rapport with the audience. The takeaway message is that your attitude is the biggest determinant of what you can accomplish—and you alone control your attitude. True innovators see their way to solutions even in very difficult circumstances.

A wonderful example is Jeff Hawkins, who began his career at Palm Computing, rethinking how people could organize their complicated lives, and is now focused on revolutionizing our understanding of how the brain works. In the early days of personal computers, Jeff was drawn to the problem of creating handheld devices that were easily accessible to the general public. This was a grand goal that required a deep understanding of technology and potential users. Along the way, he faced an endless array of challenges, and he admits that being an entrepreneur means constantly facing big problems and finding creative ways to tame them.

Jeff's challenges began at the very beginning. When Palm released its first product, the Zoomer, it failed miserably. Instead of walking away in defeat, Jeff and his team called every customer who had purchased the product, as well as many who had purchased its rival, the Apple Newton (which was also a failure), and asked what they had *hoped* the product would do. Customers said they had hoped and expected the products to help them organize their complicated schedules. That's when Jeff realized the Zoomer was competing much more with paper calendars than with other computer products. This surprising feedback, which contradicted his original assumptions, provided useful input for the design of the next-generation product, the fabulously successful PalmPilot.

The path to success was far from easy, and there were many times when Jeff and his team could have given up. But they knew that challenges are a natural part of the creative process, and they were ready when problems cropped up.

In fact, Jeff gets worried when things go too smoothly, knowing that a problem must be lurking just around the corner. When he was running his second company, Handspring, everything was going swimmingly for the release of the original Visor, a new personal digital assistant. But Jeff kept warning his team that something would happen. And it did.

Within the first few days of the release of their first product they had shipped about 100,000 units. This was a remarkable feat! But the entire billing and shipping system broke down in the process. Some customers didn't receive the products, and others received three or four times as many units as they ordered. It was a disaster, especially for a new business that was trying to build its reputation. So how did they handle it? The entire team, including Jeff, buckled down and called each and every customer. They asked each person what they had ordered, if they had received it, and whether they had been billed correctly. If anything wasn't perfect, the company corrected it on the spot. Jeff had *known* something would go wrong; he just wasn't sure what it would be. His experience has taught him that problems are inevitable, and the key to success is not dodging every bullet but recovering quickly.

Jeff's current company, Numenta, is addressing an enormous challenge head-on. He has spent years teaching himself neuroscience in an attempt to understand how we think. From his extensive research, Jeff came up with a new and provocative theory about how the neocortex in the brain processes information, which he describes in his book *On Intelligence*. With these theories in hand, Jeff used his ideas as the foundation for a "smarter" computer that processes information like the human brain does. As in all his ventures, problems crop up frequently, and he is ready to tackle them.

Of course, one could argue that Jeff Hawkins is one of a kind and that we can't all develop revolutionary theories and groundbreaking inventions. But it is much more productive to see Jeff as a source of inspiration, as someone who demonstrates that problems can be solved if we give ourselves permission to look at them differently.

• • •

One project that came out of the Innovation Tournament sheds light on how to turn problems into opportunities. Participants were challenged to create as much value as possible with rubber bands. One team came up with the idea for Do Bands, bracelets that would give people a simple incentive to "do" the things they often put off doing.[1] Do Bands was a clever idea, inspired by the now-familiar rubber bracelets worn to show solidarity with a cause. Do Bands had a few guiding principles:

- Put one around your wrist with a promise to do something.
- Take it off when you have completed the task.
- Record your success online at the Do Bands website. Each Do Band came with a number printed on it so you could look up all the actions it had inspired.
- Pass the Do Band along to someone else.

Do Bands gave individuals an incentive to do what they wanted to do all along. In reality, a Do Band was just a rubber band. However, sometimes something as simple as a rubber band is all that's needed to mobilize people to actually do something, to bridge the gap between inaction and action. The Do Bands campaign lasted only a few days, but in that short time it inspired a long list of actions: some people called their mothers, some showed their appreciation to others by sending thank-you notes, and one began a new exercise program. One participant used the Do Band as an impetus to start a summer camp, one was inspired to reach out to long-lost friends, and some donated money to charities of their choice. It's fascinating that a lowly rubber band was catalyst enough to move people to act. It's also a clear reminder that there is just a tiny gap between doing nothing and doing something, but the two options have wildly different outcomes. Lewis Pugh, an environmentalist who swam across the North Pole to bring attention to the issues facing our planet, poignantly says, "You are always one decision away from a completely different life."[2]

I assign a simple challenge in my creativity class that's designed to give students the experience of looking at obstacles in their lives from a new perspective. In this challenge I ask them to identify a problem they are facing and then pick a random object in their environment and figure out how that object will help them solve their problem. Of course, I have no notion about their personal challenges or what objects they will select. However, in most cases they manage to find a way to use random objects to tackle a seemingly unrelated problem. Selecting the object gives them permission to look at the problem differently and an incentive to find a solution.

My favorite example is a young woman who was moving from one apartment to another. She had to transport some large furniture and had no idea how to make it happen. If she couldn't move the furniture, she would have to leave it in her old apartment. She looked around her apartment and saw a case of wine that was left over from a party a few weeks earlier. Aha! She went to Craigslist, an online community bulletin board, and offered to trade the case of wine for a ride across the Bay Bridge with her furniture. Within a few hours, all of her furniture was moved! The leftover wine collecting dust in the corner had been transformed into valuable currency. The assignment gave this student the ability and motivation to see her problem as solvable.

There is no limit to the types of problems you can tackle. In fact, most of the Innovation Tournament projects are crafted to create "social value." That is, students use the competition as an opportunity to address a significant problem in our community, such as saving energy, encouraging people to stay healthy, or providing support for disabled children.

•   •   •

The first step to solving big problems is to identify them. In the world of product design, this is called "need finding," and it's a skill that can be learned. In fact, it's a key component of the curriculum for the Biodesign program at Stanford.[3] Postgraduates who have studied engineering, medicine, and business come together for a year to identify significant needs in medicine and then design products to address them. Paul Yock, a cardiologist, inventor, and entrepreneur, launched and runs the program. Paul believes that a well-characterized need is the DNA of an invention. In other words, if we clearly define a problem, the solution will logically present itself. This echoes a quote attributed to Albert Einstein: "If I had an hour to solve a problem and my life depended on the solution, I would spend the first fifty-five minutes determining the proper question to ask, for once I know the proper question, I could solve the problem in less than five minutes."

The Biodesign Fellows spend three months shadowing doctors in action and identifying problems the doctors appear to be facing. They watch carefully, talk with all of the stakeholders—

including physicians, nurses, patients, and administrators—and figure out where things can be improved. They whittle down a list of hundreds of needs to just a handful, with the goal of picking the biggest problems they have found. After they settle on the challenge, they design and quickly build prototypes for a variety of solutions. After a focused, iterative process, they present their new product concepts to the key stakeholders to find out if they have successfully met the needs.

Interestingly, in many cases those who are on the front lines of medicine are so used to the problems they experience every day that they don't even see them or can't imagine radical approaches to solving them. Paul Yock shared a story about the development of balloon angioplasty, a technique that involves inserting a balloon into an artery and expanding it to open the blocked artery. Before this breakthrough invention, most cardiologists believed that the only way to deal with clogged arteries was to do bypass surgery to remove the damaged blood vessels. This procedure required open-heart surgery, which carried substantial risks. When the balloon angioplasty procedure, which is much less dangerous and invasive, was first introduced, it was met with tremendous skepticism and resistance among physicians, especially surgeons who "understood best" how to treat the disease. Significant roadblocks appeared in front of pioneers of the procedure. For example, John Simpson, one of the inventors of balloon angioplasty, wound up having to leave his university to do his research at a private hospital. However, over time, the efficacy of balloon angioplasty was firmly established and it became the standard of care for most patients with clogged arteries. This is a great example of how the status quo can be so entrenched that those closest to the situation can't imagine anything different.

"Problem blindness" applies to consumer product development as well. For example, automatic teller machines (ATMs) failed in early focus groups in which potential customers were asked if they would use a machine to deposit and withdraw money from their accounts, as opposed to going into a local bank to complete the transaction with a teller. These customers couldn't imagine changing their behavior so dramatically. But in retrospect, ATMs represented a new and effective improvement for personal banking, one that few of us can now imagine living without.

I've experienced problem blindness myself. About twenty-five years ago my husband, Mike, gave me a cell phone. This was long before cell phones were ubiquitous, and I had no idea I needed one. In fact, I got somewhat annoyed, thinking it was one more electronic gadget that would sit around unused. Mike urged me to try it for a week. It took me only two days to figure out I couldn't live without it. I was commuting at least two hours each day and was able to catch up with friends and colleagues during the drive. I came back to Mike with sincere appreciation for the gift and now try to keep this story in mind when I look at new, potentially breakthrough ideas.

The key to need finding is identifying and filling gaps—gaps in the way people use products, gaps in the services available, and gaps in the stories people tell when interviewed about their behavior. Michael Barry, an expert in need finding, told our class a terrific story about his work with Kimberly-Clark, the company that makes Kleenex, Scott paper towels, and Huggies diapers. Essentially, Kimberly-Clark was disappointed with their diaper sales relative to diaper giants such as Procter & Gamble (makers of Pampers) and brought in Michael's team to help figure out how they could improve their business. By making detailed observations on how diapers are sold, assessing the messaging on diaper packages, and conducting interviews with parents, Michael realized that Kimberly-Clark was completely missing the point: they were selling diapers as though they were "hazardous waste disposal devices." But parents don't view them that way. To a parent, a diaper is a way to keep their children comfortable. Dealing with diapers is part of the nurturing process. A diaper is also viewed as a piece of clothing. These observations provided a great starting point for improving how Kimberly-Clark packaged and positioned Huggies.

Upon closer scrutiny, Michael identified an even *bigger* opportunity. He noticed that parents became terribly embarrassed when asked if their child was "still in diapers." Bingo! This was a huge pain point for parents and for kids on the cusp of toilet training. There had to be a way to turn this around. How could a diaper become a symbol of success as opposed to failure? Michael came up with the idea for Pull-Ups, a cross between a diaper and underwear. Switching from diapers to Pull-Ups served as a big milestone for both children and parents. A child can put on a Pull-Up without help and can feel proud of this accomplishment. This insight led to a billion-dollar increase in annual revenue for Kimberly-Clark and allowed them to leapfrog ahead of their competition. This new product grew out of focused need finding, identification of a clear problem, and the emergence of an opportunity.

In my course, I use a Harvard case study about Cirque du Soleil that gives students a chance to hone their skills at challenging assumptions.[4] The backdrop is the 1980s, when the circus industry was in trouble. Performances were predictable and stale, the number of customers was diminishing, and animal treatment was under attack. It didn't seem like a good time to start a new circus, but that is exactly what Guy Laliberté, a street performer in Canada, decided to do. Guy started Cirque du Soleil by challenging every assumption about what a circus could be, and in doing so transformed a problem—a dying industry—into an opportunity.

After showing video clips from the 1939 Marx Brothers movie *At the Circus*, I ask the students to uncover all the assumptions of a traditional circus, such as a big tent, animals, cheap tickets, barkers selling souvenirs, several acts performing at once, playful music, clowns, popcorn, strong men, flaming hoops, etc. I then ask them to turn these things upside down—to imagine the exact opposite of each one. For example, the new list would include a fixed building, no animals, expensive seats, no barkers, one act performing at a time, sophisticated music, and no clowns or popcorn. They then pick the things they want to keep from the traditional circus and the things they want to change.

The result is a brand-new type of circus, à la Cirque du Soleil. I then show them video clips from recent Cirque du Soleil performances so they can see the impact of these changes. Most important, they see how unpacking and then challenging their assumptions exposed the possibilities for a brand-new type of circus that is more in tune with today's audiences. This example illustrates one reason why the famous Ringling Bros.

and Barnum & Bailey Circus, which started in 1871 and was billed as the Greatest Show on Earth, went out of business in 2017. The company ignored the need to reinvent itself, while Cirque du Soleil challenged traditional assumptions about what a circus could be and was therefore able to thrive.

Once we do this exercise with the circus industry, it's easy to apply it to other industries and institutions, including fast-food restaurants, hotels, airlines, sporting events, education, and even courtship and marriage. Once you get the hang of it, this is an easy, back-of-the-envelope exercise you can use to reevaluate everything from breakfast to banking. The key is to take the time to clearly identify all of your assumptions. This is usually the hardest part, since, as described in the case about balloon angioplasty, assumptions are sometimes so integrated into our view of the world that it's hard to actually see them. However, with a little practice, it becomes a useful way to look at your options in a fresh light.

My colleague Rich Braden, who has taught with me for several years, decided to use this exercise while planning his recent wedding. He and his fiancée made a list of about fifty assumptions for traditional weddings, including wedding rings, formal dress, bride wearing white, wedding vows, fancy cake, professional photographer, band/DJ, and kissing the bride. They then turned all of those assumptions upside down and came up with a new list of ideas, including no rings, casual dress, wearing tie-dye, no vows, pie and ice cream, cell phone photos, karaoke, and high-fiving the bride. They then chose to keep some of the original assumptions and to change up others, crafting a celebration that was perfect for them.

This practice can be used for anything! At Stanford Sierra Camp, near Lake Tahoe, Morgan Marshall was in charge of housekeeping for many years. He decided to turn the entire process on its head, making the most hated task into the most loved one. As you can imagine, everyone on the staff dreaded having to do the dishes for the entire camp. But Morgan turned dishwashing into the most plum job. Those who wash dishes get to pick the music in the kitchen, crafting elaborate playlists to accompany the activity, and they come up with a theme and dress accordingly. I've seen people dressed as fairies, disco dancers, and cowboys. They essentially turn dishwashing into a party. Also, the staff meets frequently with the goal of coming up with more and more effective and efficient ways to do the job. Finally, there is a policy that nobody is done in the kitchen until everyone is done, so everyone is there to chip in if needed, joining the party. Amazingly, the staff eagerly looks forward to their time in the soapy bubbles.

Some people are particularly good at identifying and challenging assumptions. In their quest to find solutions to seemingly impossible problems, they question the limits of what is reasonable and possible. They start their lives over in exotic locations, they take on projects that have a grand scope, they make choices that seem radical, and they carve out a new path that leads them into uncharted territory.

Consider Anne Wojcicki, the founder of 23andMe. She challenged a tremendous number of assumptions by questioning who had access to each individual's genetic information and, after years of work, was ultimately able to provide direct-to-consumer genetic testing at 23andMe. This required challenging government regulations, challenging the way genetic testing was done, and challenging consumers to see the value in owning their own genetic information.

Or Leila Janah, the founder and CEO of Samasource, who questioned how we provide support for people in developing countries by giving them work as opposed to handouts. Instead of seeing poor people as targets for charity, she devised ways to give them work to support themselves and their families.

Or Pat Brown, the founder and CEO of Impossible Foods, who has created a vegetarian substitute for meat products. He challenged the assumption that people want to eat animal meat. He realized that people eat meat *not* because they want to kill animals but in spite of the need to kill animals. His company, Impossible Foods, reverse engineered meat to create an alternative, made entirely from plants, that is indistinguishable from ground meat.

Stories about challenging assumptions are told weekly in STVP's Entrepreneurial Thought Leaders series.[5] In each case, these entrepreneurs question the status quo and look at the world with fresh eyes. Of course, their paths are filled with potholes. But they expect this and foster a mindset that every pothole can be filled along the way, paving a path to success.

We often watch in awe, preventing ourselves from taking the same leaps. In many cases, much smaller challenges seem just as daunting. Changing jobs or moving across town may feel just as risky as traveling to an exotic location or launching a new company with a grand mission. It's much more comfortable to stay locked in a role that's "good enough" than to reach for an alternative that has a higher degree of uncertainty. Most of us are content taking small, reliable steps. We don't get very far, but we don't risk stumbling either.

• • •

If you want to consider what your life would look like upside down, consider using the challenging assumptions exercise for yourself. Make a "before" list with all of your assumptions about how you spend your time, including when you wake up each morning, the specific days and hours you work each week, the length of your commute, the type of work you do, the people with whom you work, the amount of time you exercise, with whom you spend your free time, what you eat for dinner, what you do in the evening and on the weekends, where you go for vacation, how much money you save each paycheck, how you feel at the end of the day, when you go to sleep, etc. Make the list as long as possible, unpacking as many assumptions about your life as you can.

Then consider alternatives to all of these by creating an "after" list. The items on this list should be the opposite, or an exaggeration, of the things on the "before" list. For example, if you exercise by yourself for twenty minutes each day, the alternatives would include no exercise at all, taking an exercise class at a gym, or running with a dog. And if you spend your free time watching TV or knitting, then alternatives might be volunteering at a soup kitchen, learning how to skydive, or taking an improvisation class.

Once you have your lists, mix and match from the "before" and "after" lists to craft a brand-new set of scenarios. Switching even one of the assumptions might be enough to shake up your life in an interesting way. Remember, there are boundless options to explore if you are willing to identify and challenge your assumptions. To quote Alan Alda, "Your assumptions are your windows on the world. Scrub them off every once in a while or the light won't come in."[6]

•   •   •

Despite the fact that one can make a profit by solving big problems, Randy Komisar stresses in his book *The Monk and the Riddle* the importance of having the zeal to solve an important problem, as opposed to being motivated to make money.[7] To explain the difference, he compares a missionary who passionately pursues an important cause to a mercenary whose drive is only to serve his or her own interests. By focusing on finding solutions to significant challenges with missionary-like zeal, successful companies are born. This message is echoed by author Guy Kawasaki, who says it is better to "make meaning than to make money."[8] If your goal is to make meaning by trying to solve a big problem in innovative ways, you are more likely to make money than if you start with the goal of making money, in which case you will probably not make money *or* meaning.

What do the entrepreneurs, venture capitalists, and inventors described previously have to do with the students who started with five dollars, paper clips, or orphan socks and were challenged to create as much value as possible? A tremendous amount. All of these examples reinforce the idea that there is great benefit to identifying problems in your midst and then relentlessly working to solve them. This doesn't mean that this process isn't scary—it is! There is always a risk that your endeavors

won't work out. As Elon Musk, world-famous inventor and entrepreneur, said in an interview, "I actually think I feel fear quite
strongly. . . . There are just times when something is important
enough that you believe in it enough that you do it in spite of
fear."[9]

Problems and opportunities are abundant, just waiting for
someone willing to find inventive solutions. This takes acute
observation, coordinated teamwork, the ability to execute a
plan, a willingness to learn from failure, and creative problem-
solving. But the first requirement is to have the attitude that
the problem can be solved. I have found, for myself and my students, that the more experience you have tackling problems,
the more confident you become that you can find solutions.

Several years ago I was in Scotland teaching in a weeklong
entrepreneurship boot camp, run by James Barlow at the Scottish Institute for Enterprise. Attending were fifty college students from across the country who were studying a wide range
of disciplines, from criminology to cosmetics. Most of them
had had no exposure to entrepreneurship at all. At the beginning of the week, many were completely overwhelmed by the
first assignment, which required them to come up with and
then sell a new product or service. Each team was given fifty
British pounds of starting capital at 6:00 p.m. and had a total
of eighteen hours to complete the project. The goal was to get
them out of their comfort zone and into the real world. Many
of the students told me they were on the verge of going home.
They didn't need to tell me this, because the panicked looks
on their faces said it all. But they all stuck with it and were
pleasantly shocked by what they accomplished. One group became "umbrella walkers," assisting people who got caught in

an unexpected rain; one group set up an impromptu speed-dating station at a local bar; and one started a makeshift shoe-shine stand on a busy downtown street.

But this assignment was just the beginning of their experience. By the end of a week's worth of challenging activities, including scouring newspapers to identify problems, brainstorming to come up with creative solutions, designing new ventures, meeting with potential customers, filming commercials, and pitching their ideas to a panel of successful executives, they were ready to take on just about any challenge.

One team that stands out in my mind was composed of three young women, for whom all of this was brand-new. They were shaking in their shoes when the first assignment was given. By the end of the week, however, they had come up with a fabulous idea that earned high praise from the panel of judges as well as seed funding from investors. They developed a mobile, at-home bra-fitting service based on their observation that most women are embarrassed by the process and often end up with ill-fitting bras. Their video commercial was tasteful and convinced everyone that this was an interesting opportunity.

On the last day of the workshop, one of the young women said to me, "I now know that there isn't anything I can't do." She, along with all the other students, already had the bulk of the skills they needed to accomplish amazing things. All we offered them was tangible proof, along with a healthy dose of permission, that they could turn the problems around them into opportunities.

That sentiment is echoed by Jared Lindzon in his *New York Times* article about how he beat his fear of rejection, failure, and vulnerability by literally jumping out of a perfectly good airplane with a trained skydiver.[10] In that moment he realized that by doing the scariest thing he could imagine doing, and realizing that he wouldn't die, there were few things in the world to truly fear.

Chapter 3

Bikini or Die

The famous psychologist B. F. Skinner once wrote that all human behavior can be viewed as adaptive to either the individual, the gene pool, or society at large.[1] However, these three forces are often at odds, causing significant tension. The rules made by society are a huge presence in our lives, created by the government, religious groups, employers, schools, neighbors, and families. Every day, physical signs tell all of us what to do, written instructions direct us how to behave, and social guidelines urge us to act within specific parameters. The social rules and norms are designed to make the world around us more organized and predictable, and to prevent us from hurting one another.

Because our community crafts the explicit rules around us, we often find ourselves in situations in which we are driven to break the rules to satisfy our personal desires or the drives of our species. In fact, we also make lots of rules for ourselves, in large part encouraged by others. These rules become woven into our individual fabric as we go through life. We draw imaginary lines around what we think we can do—lines that often limit us much more than the rules imposed by society at large. We define ourselves by our profession, our income, where we live, the car we drive, our education, and even by our horoscope. Each definition locks us into specific assumptions about who we are and what we can do. I'm reminded of a famous line from the movie *My Dinner with Andre* that states that New Yorkers "are both guards and prisoners, and as a result they no longer have . . . the capacity to leave the prison they've made, or to even see it as a prison."[2] We often make our own prisons, with rules we each create for ourselves, locking us into specific roles and out of an endless array of possibilities.

But when is a rule really just a suggestion? And when do suggestions morph into rules? What if you challenge the underlying assumptions? What are the consequences—good and bad—of getting off the prescribed path? What happens to those who break the rules?

Larry Page, cofounder of Google, gave a lecture in which he encouraged the audience to break free from established guidelines by having a healthy disregard for the impossible.[3] That is, to think as big as possible. He noted that it is often easier to have big goals than to have small goals. With small goals, there are very specific ways to reach them and more ways they can go wrong. With big goals, you are usually allocated more resources, and there are more ways to achieve them. This is an interesting insight. Imagine that you are trying to get from San Francisco to the South Pole. There are lots of different routes, you will likely give yourself the time and resources to get there, and you will be flexible if things don't unfold as planned. But if your goal is to go across town, then the path is pretty clear and you expect it to be a quick trip. If the road is blocked for some reason, you're stuck and frustrated.

Linda Rottenberg is a prime example of a person who sees no problem as too big to tackle and readily breaks free of expectations in order to get where she wants to go. She believes that if others think your ideas are crazy, then you must be on the right track. Twenty years ago Linda started a remarkable organization called Endeavor.[4] Its goal is to foster entrepreneurship in the developing world. She launched Endeavor just after graduating from Yale Law School, with little more than a passion to stimulate economic development in disadvantaged regions. She stopped at nothing to reach her goals, including "stalking" influential business leaders whose support she needed.

Endeavor began its efforts in Latin America and has since expanded to other regions of the world, including Turkey and South Africa. The organization goes through a rigorous process to identify high-potential entrepreneurs and, after selecting those with great ideas and the drive to execute their plans, gives them the resources they need to be successful. The entrepreneurs are not handed money but instead introduced to those in their environment who can guide them. They are also provided with educational programs and get an opportunity to meet with other entrepreneurs in their region who have navigated the circuitous path before. Once successful, they serve as positive role models, create jobs in their local communities, and eventually give back to Endeavor, helping future generations of entrepreneurs.

An inspiring example of an Endeavor entrepreneur is Leila Velez in Brazil. Leila lived in the slums, known as favelas, in the hills overlooking Rio de Janeiro. Cleaning houses, she survived on a subsistence income. However, she had an idea. There are many women in Brazil who want desperately to have softer, less kinky hair. Leila, along with her sister-in-law, Heloísa Assis, invented a product that transforms knotty hair into curly hair. It took years of trial-and-error experimentation, resulting in many extreme failures along the way, but once she found a solution, she opened a salon in Rio. Her business was brisk, and Leila had the fantasy of creating a franchise. Along came Endeavor, which helped her realize her dream. With Endeavor's support and guidance, this business, called Beleza Natural, now employs three thousand people, has more than fifty different products, and earns millions in annual revenue.

This is but one of hundreds of success stories from Endeavor. I was at Endeavor's biannual summit several years ago and was overwhelmed with the energy and enthusiasm in the room. Each entrepreneur was indebted to Endeavor for providing the tools they needed as well as the inspiration to succeed. This would never have happened if Linda had listened to the people who told her that her ideas were crazy. In fact, since then Linda has written a book about her experience, called *Crazy Is a Compliment.*

One of the biggest obstacles to taking on "impossible tasks" is that others are often quick to tell you they can't be accomplished. This is exactly what happened to Nicolas Shea when he decided to take on a challenge that seemed impossible. It was 2012, and Nico had recently founded Start-Up Chile and was launching a new peer-to-peer lending platform in Chile, called Cumplo. Just three months after launching this new venture, they hit a big snag. The country banking supervisor threatened him with prison if he continued his business.[5] He realized that banking regulations in Chile were designed to protect the large, established banks and left no room for innovation for entrepreneurs who wanted to find ways to improve the system.

Nico looked at this dilemma from all different angles and finally realized the only way to change the system was to get the more open-minded individuals into political positions. He decided to explore how one actually runs for office. It became clear that unless you were sponsored by an established party, it was a daunting process, requiring painful bureaucracy, paperwork, time, and money. No wonder so few people were willing or able to run for office.

Nico had a crazy idea: What if any citizen could become a politician? He cooked up the idea of creating a Cumplo-like platform for politics so anyone could easily declare and fund a campaign. Inspired by this idea, Nico decided to start a brand-new political party, called Todos, meaning "everyone" in Spanish. The values of the party were simple—honesty, collaboration, respect, transparency, and accountability—and anyone in the country could declare themselves a candidate.

To become an official party, they needed 35,000 signatures, and each of those signatures needed to be officially notarized by one of the very few notaries in the country. So, what did he do? He literally stood in front of the notary offices with a clipboard in different cities, talked with everyone who walked by, and asked them to sign up for this new multi-ideology party. With this tactic, he was able to get enough signatures to get the party on the official ballot in four of the fifteen regions of the country.

The next step was to get candidates to sign up to run. The first person to accept this challenge was a famous comedian and radio host in Chile. This was great, but they needed more candidates to demonstrate they were serious. So, after agonizing about it for quite some time, Nico decided to step down as president of the party to run himself!

On March 1, 2017, Nico became an official "pre-candidate for president" in Chile. He stopped everything he was doing and took on this new role, traveling the country and talking with citizens from diverse backgrounds to understand their perspectives. Todos also attracted fourteen other candidates, seven for senate seats and seven for congress.

Many people close to Nico thought he was completely nuts! His wife, mother, and teenage daughter begged him to quit. But he knew he needed to demonstrate that for democracy to work, everyone could and should get involved in the governing of the country. He was never more afraid. In fact, when a friend asked him if he knew what he was getting into, he burst into tears. He knew he had to take this on, but he also knew it would be the most challenging thing he did in his life.

Although nobody in the Todos party won in their political races and the party didn't meet the minimum votes to continue, Nico is incredibly proud that they all tried, and he plans to rebuild the party again soon. This example illustrates that if you set an enormous goal for yourself—like democratizing democracy—you must break it down into concrete steps to overcome the inevitable hurdles along the way.

•   •   •

It is arguably a huge endeavor to address a grand problem. But once you decide to take it on, it is equally hard to challenge traditional approaches to solving that problem. This is another place where it is helpful to break a few rules.

One of my favorite classroom exercises turns problem-solving on its head. First, I come up with a problem that is relevant for the particular group. For example, if it is a group of executives in the utility business, the topic might be getting companies to save energy; if it is a theater group, the problem might be how to attract a larger audience; and if it is a group of students, the challenge might be to come up with ideas for a brand-new restaurant. Then I break the group into teams and ask each team to come up with the *best* ideas and the *worst* ideas for solving the stated problem. The best ideas are approaches that each team thinks will solve the problem brilliantly. The worst ideas will be ineffective or unprofitable or make the problem worse. Once the teams are finished, they write their *best* best ideas on a separate piece of paper, labeled BEST, and their *worst* worst ideas on one labeled WORST. I then ask the participants to pass both to me. I read the best ideas out loud—which are usually pretty incremental, such as a restaurant on the top of a mountain with a beautiful sunset—and then shred them. The students are clearly shocked and none too happy.

I then redistribute the worst ideas. Each team now has an idea that another team thought was terrible. They are instructed to turn this bad idea into a fabulous idea. They look at the horrible idea passed their way and quickly see that the idea has a seed of brilliance. Within a few seconds, someone always says, "Hey, this is a great idea!"

When doing this exercise with a utility company, one of the "worst" ideas for saving energy was to give each employee a quota for how much energy he or she used and to charge extra for exceeding the allotment. They thought this was a pretty silly idea. The team that received this "bad" idea turned it into one worth considering. Employees would be given a quota for how much energy they use. If they use less, they get money back, and if they use more, they are charged for it. They could also sell energy credits to their coworkers, giving them an even larger incentive to save electricity. They essentially set up a program that is similar to the cap-and-trade model used by some companies.

I did this exercise with the staff responsible for putting on arts events at Stanford. One of the teams charged with finding ways to bring in a larger audience came up with the "bad" idea of putting on a Stanford staff talent show. This is seemingly the opposite of what they do now—bringing in top-notch talent from around the world. The next team turned this idea upside down. They interpreted this much more broadly and proposed a big fund-raiser, during which the faculty and staff across the university would showcase their diverse talents. This would very likely bring in lots of people who wouldn't normally go to performing arts events and would help build awareness for their other programs.

When the challenge was to come up with the worst business idea, the suggestions were boundless. One group suggested selling bikinis in Antarctica, one recommended starting a restaurant that sells cockroach sushi, and one group proposed starting a heart attack museum. In each of these cases, these bad ideas were transformed into pretty interesting ideas that deserved some real consideration. For example, the group that was tasked with selling bikinis in Antarctica came up with the slogan "Bikini or Die." Their idea was to take people who wanted to get into shape on a trip to Antarctica. By the end of the hard journey, they would be able to fit into their bikinis. The group that needed to sell cockroach sushi came up with a restaurant called La Cucaracha that made all sorts of exotic sushi using nontraditional but nutritious ingredients and targeted adventurous diners. The group given the challenge of starting a heart attack museum used this idea as the starting point for a museum devoted entirely to health and preventative medicine. All groups came up with compelling business names, slogans, and commercials for these ventures.

This exercise is a great way to open your mind to solutions to problems because it demonstrates that most ideas, even if they look silly or stupid on the surface, often have a seed of potential. The "good" ideas are usually expected and incremental, but the "bad" ideas open the door to some truly unique solutions. More important, it demonstrates that with the right frame of mind you can look at most ideas or situations and find something valuable. For example, even if you don't start the "Bikini or Die" excursion to Antarctica, this is an interesting jumping-off point for ideas that might be more practical.

My old buddy John Stiggelbout used the notion of turning a good idea on its head when applying to graduate school. He did something any normal person would think was a terribly bad idea, and it turned out to be inspired. He decided at the last minute that he wanted to go to business school. Having missed all the deadlines, he chose to make his application stand out among the others in an unconventional way. Instead of touting his impressive accomplishments, he asked a former professor of his to write a humorous letter, claiming to be John's best friend and cellmate in prison. The letter described John in the most colorful terms that any admissions committee had ever seen, including his ability to open a mason jar with his belch. Instead of knocking John out of the running, those in the admissions office were incredibly curious to meet this audacious candidate and invited John to visit the school. John was nice enough to dig up the letter so you can see it, too.

I met John Stiggelbout as a fellow Greyhound bus passenger. He must have passed out on the floor at the back. I found him next to a Styrofoam cup and a candy wrapper, covered with cigarette butts, holding an empty MD 20/20 bottle. I am his best friend. We were cellmates after we got caught robbing the 7-Eleven. After a hearty meal at the Salvation Army, we once went to a revival meeting where we were both trying to pick up the same girl. (He takes defeat and humiliation well; he is obviously a practiced loser.)

He has impressive qualities that any struggling Junior Achievement Company or small family laundry could put to good use. He covers his brown and yellow teeth when he yawns and opens the window when he spits. He can whistle loud using his fingers and can crack a mason jar with his burp. He showers once a month. He uses soap when he can. He needs a place so he doesn't have to sleep in the bus station restroom. He needs to find a position with a large company where his heavy drinking and sexual preference for exotic birds will not get him fired the first day on the job. Anyone with a sexual preference for exotic birds is both original and independent of thought. In fact, he is so independent of thought that he is utterly devoid of it.

This guy will do anything for a drink. He may even work. Now that Stiggs is out of jail, I'm sure his parole officer would not mind if some graduate school looked after him for a bit. He is a great leader in the Hell's Angels, and all the boys I talked to thought he would make a hell of a white-collar criminal. Of all the people I have found on the floor, passed out in the back of a bus, this guy is the best. My overall impression is that he is not as good as I make him out to be. Get me out of jail so that I can go to Chicago instead of him.

BUFORD T. MORTON, INMATE #335342
WALLA WALLA STATE PENITENTIARY
WALLA WALLA, WASHINGTON

Once John arrived for the interview, everyone in the office was peeking out of his or her door, hoping to get a look at the fellow who submitted the application. He was polite and poised during his interview, and was admitted.

• • •

The concept that there are no bad ideas is a hallmark of good brainstorming. Sometimes the craziest ideas, which seem impractical when they are initially proposed, turn out to be the most interesting in the long run. They might not work in their first iteration, but with a bit of massaging, they might turn out to be brilliant solutions that are feasible to implement.

Running a successful brainstorming session actually takes a lot of skill and practice. You need to explicitly state it is essential to break with the assumption that ideas need to be feasible in order to be valuable. By encouraging people to come up with wild ideas, you defuse the tendency to edit them before they are shared. The key is to set the ground rules at the beginning and to reinforce them. Tom Kelley, a partner at the design firm IDEO and David Kelley's brother, wrote a book called *The Art of Innovation*, in which he describes the rules of brainstorming at their firm. One of the most important rules is to expand upon the ideas of others. With this approach, at the end of a good brainstorming session, multiple people feel they have created or contributed to the best ideas to come out of the session. And since everyone in the room had a chance to participate and witnessed the emergence and evolution of all the ideas, there is usually shared support for the ideas that go forward toward implementation.

If you have participated in brainstorming sessions, you know that they don't always work like that. It's hard to eliminate the natural tendency for each person to feel personal ownership for their ideas, and it can be tough to get participants to build on others' suggestions. Patricia Ryan Madson, author of *Improv Wisdom*, designed a great warm-up exercise that reinforces these two ideas: there are no bad ideas *and* build on others' ideas. You break a group into pairs. One person tries to plan a party and makes suggestions to the other person. The other person has to say no to every idea and must give a reason why it won't work. For example, the first person might say, "Let's plan a party for Saturday night," and the second person would say, "No, I have to wash my hair." This goes on for a few minutes, as the first person continues to get more and more frustrated trying to come up with any idea the second person will accept.

Once this runs its course, the roles switch and the second person takes on the job of planning a party. The first person has to say yes to everything and must build on the idea. For example, "Let's have a party on Saturday night." The response might be, "Yes, and I'll bring a cake." This goes on for a while, and the ideas can get pretty wild. In some cases the parties end up underwater or on another planet and involve all sorts of exotic food and entertainment. The energy in the room increases, spirits are high, and a huge number of ideas are generated.

This is the type of energy that should be present during a great brainstorming session. Of course, at some point you have to decide what is feasible, but that shouldn't happen during the idea-generation phase. Brainstorming is about breaking out of conventional approaches to solving a problem. You should feel free to flip ideas upside down, to turn them inside out, and to cut loose from the chains of normalcy. At the end of a brainstorming session you should be surprised by the range of ideas that were generated. In almost all cases at least a few will serve as the seeds for really great opportunities that are ripe for further exploration.

It is important to remember that idea generation involves "exploration" of the landscape of possibilities. It doesn't cost any money to generate a wide variety of ideas, and there is no need to commit to any of them. The goal is to break the rules by imagining a world where the laws of nature are different and all constraints are removed. Once this phase is complete, it is appropriate to move on to the "exploitation" phase, in which you evaluate the ideas and select some to explore further. At that time you can view the ideas with a more critical eye.

Rule breaking can happen throughout every organization and in all processes. Consider companies such as Lyft, Airbnb, Netflix, and SpaceX, which all challenged long-held, traditional assumptions in their respective industries. Lyft challenged many assumptions about local transportation, such as people would not get into cars with strangers. Airbnb challenged the assumption that people would not want to rent out a bed or a room in their own house to a stranger. Netflix challenged the assumption that a movie distributor could not create its own content. And SpaceX challenged the assumption that space exploration should be run by governments as opposed to private companies. All of these ventures have shaken up their respective industries, opening the door to a wealth of opportunities.

Rules are often meant to be broken. This idea is captured in the oft-used phrase "Don't ask for permission, but beg for forgiveness." Most rules are in place as the lowest common denominator, making sure that those who don't have a clue what to do stay within the boundaries. If you ask someone how to go about making a movie, starting a company, getting into graduate school, running for political office, or publishing a book, you will usually get a long recipe that involves getting incrementally more support from professionals who are already in these fields. It involves agents and seed funding and exams and approvals.

The majority of people choose to follow these rules . . . but a few others don't. It's important to keep in mind that there are often creative ways to work around the rules, to jump over the traditional hurdles, and to get to a goal by taking a side route. Just as most people wait in a never-ending line of traffic on the main route to the highway, others who are a bit more adventurous try to find side roads to get to their destinations more quickly. Of course, some rules are in place to protect our safety, to keep order, and to create a process that works for a large number of people. But it is worth questioning rules along the way. Sometimes side roads around the rules can get a person to their goal even when the traditional paths appear blocked.

Linda Rottenberg of Endeavor shared an instructive story that had been passed on to her by one of her advisors, about two student fighter pilots who got together to share what they had learned from their respective instructors. The first pilot said, "I was given a thousand rules for flying my plane." The second pilot said, "I was given only three rules." The first pilot gloated, thinking he had been given many more options, until his friend said, "My instructor told me the three things I should *never* do. All else is up to me." This story captures the idea that it is better to know the few things that are really against the rules than to focus on the many things you think you should do. This is also a reminder of the big difference between rules and recommendations. Once you whittle away the recommendations, there are often many fewer rules than you imagined. This is how Linda leads Endeavor: each franchise is given three things they can't do—the rest is completely up to them.

•   •   •

Let's step out of the high-technology business world and see how you can break rules in order to create something of great value in a completely different arena. For example, the past decade has seen growing interest in restaurants that look at food, cooking, and dining in a brand-new way. Instead of using traditional cooking techniques, a new generation of chefs has been experimenting with "molecular gastronomy," which involves stretching the limits of cooking in all sorts of unusual directions. These restaurants use equipment and materials straight out of a laboratory and play with your senses in surprising ways. The kitchen might be stocked with balloons, syringes, and dry ice, and the goal is to create food that is shocking yet tasty. At Moto in Chicago, they had a "tasting menu," and you actually ate the menu, which might, for example, have tasted like an Italian panini sandwich.

The chefs at Moto strived to break the rules with each dish they served, from "delivering" FedEx boxes to the table with food that looked like packing peanuts, to making a dessert that looked like nachos but was really made up of chocolate, frozen shredded mango, and cheesecake. Each dish was designed to push the boundary of how you imagined food should look and taste as they transmogrified your food into unusual shapes and forms. One of Moto's chefs, Ben Roche, said their goal was to create a circus for your senses. They questioned every assumption about food preparation and presentation, developed brand-new cooking techniques, and even designed custom utensils used to consume the food. This is a great reminder that in any arena, from your kitchen to your career, you can remove the constraints that might be comfortable but are often limiting.

Another way to defy the rules is to break free of expectations you have for yourself and that others have for you. We each grow up with a story that others tell us and that we tell ourselves about what we can and can't do, or should or shouldn't do. I see this every day with my students. They are all in the same place, and yet they have very different aspirations based on the stories they tell themselves about how their lives will unfold. When they are encouraged to break free from self-imposed constraints, they find the range of options expands tremendously.

I met with a dozen current and former students and asked them to share their stories about breaking free from expectations. After listening to all their tales about getting around obstacles in school, in the workplace, and when traveling, one student, who graduated a few years ago, summarized all he heard by stating, "All the cool stuff happens when you do things that are not the automatic next step." The well-worn path is there for everyone to trample. But the interesting things often occur when you are open to taking an unexpected turn, trying something different, and when you are willing to question the rules others have made for you. All the students agreed that it is easy to stay on the prescribed path, but it is often much more interesting to discover the world of surprises lurking just around the corner.

Knowing that you can question the rules is terrifically empowering and a reminder that the traditional path is just one option available to you. You can always follow a recipe, drive on the major thoroughfares, and walk in the footsteps of those who came before you. But there are boundless additional options to explore if you are willing to identify and challenge assumptions and break free of the expectations you and others project onto you. Don't be afraid to get out of your comfort zone, to have a healthy disregard for the impossible, and to turn well-worn ideas on their heads. As the students described earlier learned, it takes practice to do things that are not the automatic next step. The more you experiment, the more you see that the spectrum of options is much broader than imagined. You are limited only by your energy and imagination.

Chapter 4

Please Take Out
Your Wallets

Before retiring, my father was a successful corporate executive. He rose up through the ranks, from young engineer to manager to executive, and had senior roles at several large multinational companies. Growing up, I got used to learning that he had received promotions, from vice president to executive vice president to senior executive vice president, and so on. It happened like clockwork every two years or so. I was always impressed by my father's accomplishments and viewed him as a wonderful role model.

That said, I couldn't have been more startled when my father got annoyed with me after I showed him one of my new business cards. They read TINA L. SEELIG, PRESIDENT. I had started my own company and printed my own business cards. My father looked at the cards and then at me and said, "You can't just call yourself president." In his experience, you had to wait for someone else to promote you to a leadership role. You couldn't appoint yourself. He was so steeped in a world where others promote you to positions of greater responsibility that the thought of my anointing myself perturbed him.

I have come across this mentality time and again. For example, thirty years ago when I told a friend I was going to write my first book, she asked, "What makes you think you can write a book?" She couldn't imagine taking on such a project without the blessing of someone in a position of greater authority. I, on the other hand, felt confident I could do it. The task was certainly ambitious, but why not try? At the time, there weren't any popular books on the chemistry of cooking. I wanted to read such a book, and since there wasn't one available, I decided to write one myself. I wasn't an expert on the topic, but as a scientist, I figured I could learn the material along the way. I put together a detailed proposal, wrote some sample chapters, shopped it around, and landed a contract with *Scientific American*.

After that book came out, I was disappointed by how little promotion my publisher did, and I decided to start a business to help authors get more exposure for their work and to help readers learn about books that might interest them. Again, many people asked me what made me think I could start a company. This was clearly a stretch for me, but I assumed I could figure it out. I started BookBrowser in 1991, several years before the web was born. The idea was to create a kiosk-based system for bookstore customers that would "match books with buyers." I built the prototype on my Mac computer using HyperCard, a program that allowed users to create links between cards, just like links on the web today. Users could then follow links for a particular author, title, or genre. I also met with local bookstore managers, who agreed to put the kiosks in their stores, and I talked with dozens of publishers, who were enthusiastic about including their books in the system. Satisfied that the idea was sound, I hired a team of programmers to implement the product. Nobody told me I could or should do this. I just did it.

Over time, I've become increasingly aware that the world is divided into people who wait for others to give them permission to do the things they want to do and people who grant themselves permission. Some look inside themselves for motivation and others wait to be pushed forward by outside forces. From my experience, there's a lot to be said for seizing opportunities instead of waiting for someone to hand them to you. There are always white spaces ready to be filled and golden nuggets of opportunity lying on the ground waiting for someone to pick them up. Sometimes it means looking beyond your own desk, outside your building, across the street, or around the corner. But the nuggets are there for the taking by anyone willing to gather them up.

This is exactly what Paul Yock discovered. Paul, as previously introduced, is the director of Stanford's Biodesign program. His home base is the medical school, which is literally across the street from the engineering school. Paul realized that Stanford was missing a huge opportunity by not finding ways for the medical school community to work with the engineering community to invent new medical technologies. The medical folks, including doctors, students, and research scientists, needed engineers to design new products and processes to improve patient care, and the engineers across the street were looking for compelling problems to solve using their skills.

Over the course of many months, the various stakeholders met to discuss ways they could work together. It was a complicated process since the two groups worked so differently and used very different vocabularies. Eventually they hammered out a plan and the Biodesign program was born. During the same time period, other colleagues in different medical and technical disciplines developed similar partnerships, and the groups were gathered under one large umbrella, known as Bio-X. The idea was so big that it took several years to implement and resulted in productive cross-disciplinary collaboration and a stunning new building that now stands on campus. To date, this program has developed hundreds of valuable medical devices and helped launch forty-seven new companies, which are dramatically improving the quality of life for patients around the world. This story illustrates the fact that sometimes opportunities can be found right across the street—you just have to look up from your desk to see them. Nobody told Paul to do this. But he saw the need and filled it.

•   •   •

One of the best ways to get off the prescribed path is to figure out how your skills can be translated into different settings. Others might not see the parallels on the surface, so it's your job to expose them. Sometimes the vocabulary in two disparate fields is completely different, but the job functions are remarkably similar. Consider the similarities between being a scientist and a management consultant. Soon after earning my PhD in neuroscience, I set my sights on working in a startup biotechnology company. The only problem? I wanted a job in marketing and strategy, not in a lab. This seemed nearly impossible without any relevant experience. The startup companies with which I met were looking for individuals who could hit the ground running. I interviewed for months and months and often got close to job offers, but none came through.

Eventually I got an introduction to the managing director of the San Francisco branch of Booz Allen Hamilton (known also as Booz Allen), an international consulting company.[1] My goal was to impress him enough that he would introduce me to some of the company's life-science clients. I walked into the meeting and he asked me why someone with a PhD in neuroscience would be a good management consultant. I could have told him the truth—that I actually hadn't considered that option. But on the spot, with nothing to lose, I outlined the similarities between brain research and management consulting. For example, in both cases you need to identify the burning questions, collect relevant data, analyze it, select the most interesting results, craft a compelling presentation, and determine the next set of burning questions. He was impressed enough to arrange for six more interviews that day, and I walked out that evening with a job offer!

Of course, I took it. In fact, it turned out to be an amazing way to learn about business strategy in a wide range of industries, and I certainly did leverage my prior training as a scientist. Out of necessity and curiosity, I've done this again and again, constantly reframing my skills to create new opportunities. When people ask me how a neuroscientist ended up teaching entrepreneurship to engineers, I have to say, "It's a long story."

Another way to anoint yourself is to look at things others have discarded and find ways to turn them into something useful. There is often tremendous value in the projects others have carelessly abandoned. As discussed previously, sometimes people jettison ideas because they don't fully appreciate their value or because they don't have time to fully explore them. Often these discarded ideas hold a lot of promise.

Michael Dearing started his career in strategy at Disney, went on to launch a retail venture that failed, and then landed at eBay, the leading online auction website. Michael was initially assigned to a job he wasn't thrilled about and decided to use his free time to look at features that had been designed but then ignored or abandoned—ideas just waiting for someone to exploit them. It was the year 2000, and Michael saw that there was a new feature that let customers add a photo to their standard listing for an additional twenty-five cents. Only 10 percent of eBay customers were using this feature. Michael spent some time analyzing the benefits of this service and was able to demonstrate that products with accompanying photos sold faster and at a higher price than products without photos. Armed with this compelling data, he started marketing the photo service more heavily and ended up increasing the adoption rate of this feature by customers from 10 percent to 60 percent. This resulted in $300 million in additional annual revenue for eBay. Without any instructions from others, Michael found an untapped gold mine and exploited it with great results. The cost to the company was minimal and the profits were profound.

This wasn't the first time Michael found a way to tap into resources around him. Even as a kid he wrote letters to famous people and was pleased to see that most of the time they wrote back. He still continues that habit, sending unsolicited emails to people he admires. In almost every instance they respond, and in many cases the correspondence results in long-term relationships and interesting opportunities. He never asks the folks he writes to for anything. His initial contact is all about thanking them for something they've done, acknowledging something they've accomplished, asking a simple question, or offering to help them in some way. He doesn't wait for an invitation to contact these people but takes it upon himself to make the first move.

• • •

Essentially, when you get a job—any job—you aren't given just that job but rather the keys to the building. It's up to you to decide where the keys will take you. If you *just* do the job assigned to you, you are telling your colleagues that you have reached the peak of your drive and abilities, and you will continue to do the same thing year after year. *But* if you make the effort to find ways for the organization to be more successful, you demonstrate that you are ready for bigger challenges.

So how do you find holes that need to be filled? It's actually quite simple. The first step is learning how to pay attention. My colleagues at the d.school developed the following exercise, which gets to the heart of identifying opportunities. Participants are asked to take out their wallets. They then break up into pairs and interview one another about their wallets. They discuss what they love and hate about their wallets, paying particular attention to how they use them for purchasing and storage.

One of the most interesting insights comes from watching each person pull out his or her wallet at the beginning. Some of the wallets are trim and neat, some are practically exploding with papers, some are fashion statements, some carry the individual's entire library of photos and receipts, and some consist of little more than a paper clip. Clearly, a wallet plays a different role for each of us. The interview process exposes how each person uses his or her wallet, what it represents, and the strange behaviors each person has developed to get around the wallet's limitations. I've never seen a person who is completely satisfied with his or her wallet; there is always something that can be fixed. In fact, most people are walking around with wallets that drive them crazy in some way. They discuss their frustrations with the size of their wallet, their inability to find things easily, or their desire to have different types of wallets for different occasions.

After the interview process, each person designs and builds a new wallet for the other person—his or her "customer." The design materials include nothing more than paper, tape, markers, scissors, paper clips, and the like. They can also use whatever else they find in the room. This takes about thirty minutes. After they've completed the prototype, they "sell" it to their customer. Almost universally, the new wallet solves the biggest problems with which the customer was struggling. They're thrilled with the concept and say that if that wallet were available, they would buy it. Some of the features are based on science fiction, such as a wallet that prints money on demand, but some require little more than a good designer to make them feasible right away.

Many lessons fall out of this exercise. First, the wallet is symbolic of the fact that problems are everywhere, even in your back pocket. Second, it doesn't take much effort to uncover these problems. In fact, people are generally happy to tell you about their problems. Third, by experimenting, you get quick-and-dirty feedback on the solutions you propose. It doesn't take much work, many resources, or much time. And finally, if you aren't on the right track with a solution, the sunk cost is really low. All you have to do is start over.[2]

I've run this exercise with small groups, with large groups, with kids, with doctors, and with business executives, and I switch up the prompt from wallets to umbrellas to name tags. It works with anything. In all cases they're surprised that there are always things that can be improved—from wallets and umbrellas to software, restaurants, gas stations, cars, clothes, coffee shops . . . the list is endless. You don't need someone else to give you this assignment. In fact, all successful entrepreneurs do this naturally. They pay attention at home, at work, at the grocery store, in airplanes, at the beach, at the doctor's office, or on the baseball field, and find an array of opportunities to fix things that are broken.

The wallet exercise focuses on product design. But you can use the same approach to rethink services, experiences, and organization structures. At the d.school, the teaching teams craft projects that challenge students to completely rethink a wide range of experiences, from primary school education in the United States to irrigation of crops in rural India and management of innovative organizations. If you study each situation with an eye for improvement, you will find countless opportunities. It is then up to you to decide if you will put yourself in a position to take on that challenge.

Some people are masters at taking on challenges and seizing leadership roles. I learned a lot about this from David

Rothkopf, author and CEO of The Rothkopf Group, a Washington, DC–based international advisory firm, whose book *Superclass* focuses on those people in the world who have more power and influence than the rest of us.[3] David studies leaders who've made it to the inner circle, interacting with one another in the elite World Economic Forum, which meets annually in Davos, Switzerland. I asked David what sets these people apart from the rest of us. He echoed many of the things that others in this book mentioned: people who get to the top work harder than those around them, have more energy that propels them forward, and are markedly more driven to get there. He notes that in the past people in the inner circle inherited their wealth and access. But today that isn't the case. The majority of people who claim great success have made it happen on their own. This means that the primary barriers to success are self-imposed. The corollary to this is, as David says, "the biggest ally of superachievers is the inertia of others."

David actually embodies these characteristics himself, naturally seizing opportunities, as opposed to waiting for others to hand them to him. His first company was called International Media Partners, and one of their activities was organizing conferences for top CEOs. The looming question for this startup was how to get all those exclusive and elusive executives in the same room. David and his partners needed a tempting hook and decided that getting former secretary of state Henry Kissinger to speak would do the trick. But how would they get Henry Kissinger to participate? David found out how to reach Kissinger's office and asked Kissinger's staff if he was available to speak at the conference. No problem . . . but it would cost

$50,000 and require a private airplane with two pilots and a chauffeured limousine.

David and his team didn't have any money, so any amount was too much—but he said, "Yes, we'll do it." He assumed that if he could get Henry Kissinger in the room, then the rest would fall neatly into place—and it did! Once Kissinger accepted, they were able to secure Alexander Haig, secretary of state under President Reagan; then Edmund Muskie, secretary of state under Jimmy Carter; followed by a long list of other well-known speakers. With this list of luminaries, the CEOs showed up in droves and the company was able to get sponsors that more than paid for all the speaking fees. The fact that David didn't know Henry Kissinger and had no money didn't get in his way. He succeeded by creatively leveraging what he did have: his energy, his willingness to work hard, and his drive to make it happen.

The story goes on from there. David's colleague at International Media Partners, Jeffrey Garten, went on to become undersecretary of commerce during the first Clinton administration. He invited David to become deputy undersecretary of commerce for international trade. It seemed like a pretty plum position. He had a huge office and a big staff. But after two weeks David walked into Jeff's office and quit. He couldn't stand the bureaucratic environment. Everything was painfully slow, and David was impatient to make things happen. Jeff took David outside for a walk and told him the following joke:

There was once a man named Goldberg who wanted nothing more than to be rich. So each day he went to the synagogue and prayed to God to win the lottery. This went on for days, weeks, months, and years, but Goldberg never won. Eventually Goldberg was at his wits' end. Praying to God, he said, "You have really let me down." Suddenly the silence was broken and God responded in a booming voice, "Goldberg, you've got to help me out here. You could at least buy a ticket!"

Jeff reminded David of something David already knew: he wasn't going to "win the lottery" in Washington if he didn't engage. Nobody was going to hand him the tools to be successful. So David went back to his office and tapped into his natural instincts to make things happen, as opposed to waiting for someone to show up with a game plan. He quickly realized there were endless holes to be filled and tremendous resources at his disposal. In a wonderful finale, several years after David left the Department of Commerce he became the managing director of Kissinger Associates, Inc. He went from being a newcomer who dreamed of being in the same room with Henry Kissinger to joining him as a business partner.

David has seen this story play out again and again in his own life and in the lives of those he studied while researching his book. Those who are successful find ways to make themselves successful. There is no recipe, no secret handshake, and no magic potion. Each person he studied has a story as unique as a fingerprint. The consistent theme is that they each pay attention to current trends and leverage their own skills to build their influence. They find ways to sway history, as opposed to waiting for history to sway them.

• • •

There is considerable research showing that those willing to stretch the boundaries of their current skills and willing to risk trying something new are much more likely to be successful than those who believe they have a fixed skill set and innate abilities that lock them into specific roles. Carol Dweck, in Stanford's psychology department, has written extensively about this, demonstrating that those of us with a fixed mindset about what we're good at are much less likely to be successful in the long run than those with a growth mindset. Her work focuses on our attitude about ourselves. Those with a fixed image about what they can do are much less likely to take risks that might shake that image. But those with a growth mindset are typically open to taking risks and tend to work harder to reach their objectives. They're willing to try new things that push their abilities, opening up entirely new arenas along the way.

Much of this begins by setting your objective. You can start anywhere and then craft a story about how you will get to where you want to go. I came up with an exercise for my students that helps them do this. It is called a PHD—Professional Happiness Design. Essentially, it focuses on where you are, where you want to go, and how you will get there. Some of the prompts include:

What are your core values?
What are your priorities?
What are your strongest skills?
What inspires and motivates you?

What are your short-term goals?

What are your long-term objectives?

What are your wildest dreams?

Who will be on your personal advisory board?

Who are your role models?

What knowledge do you need to build?

What skills do you need to learn?

What qualities would you like to develop?

Essentially, by understanding where you are now and set-ting goals for yourself, you set the stage for achieving them. This is exactly what Bonny Simi did. At the age of fourteen, inspired by a speaker who came to her school and shared his bold to-do list, she made up her own list of goals, including going to a good college, going to the Olympics, working as a TV reporter, and becoming a pilot. She did *all* of these things, checking them off one by one!

Accomplishing these goals was far from obvious for Bonny. She was raised by a single mother, grew up in a rural town in California, and was on public assistance. But as she says, "You have to have a dream for that dream to come true." She set her intentions early and then found ways to catch the wind that would take her there.

For example, how did she get to the Olympics? She started by applying to be an Olympic torchbearer in 1980, using her college essay as the starting point, and was accepted to repre-sent California. Since she had taken off a quarter from college to participate in the Olympics, she had a bunch of free time after the games were over. Bonny decided to take a beginning luge class that was offered for eight dollars. She found that it was a sport she could learn. So, with no experience but lots of determination, she traveled to Germany to train with some of the best luge coaches. Nobody invited her—she just showed up. Thinking she must know what she was doing, the coaches allowed her to train with the German national team. After she crashed fifty-two times in a row, she finally started to get the hang of it and improved a small amount each day. When she returned to the United States three months later, she was the best luge athlete in the country and was ultimately awarded a spot on the US national team during the 1984 Winter Olympics. Bonny used the same tools—setting a bold intention, finding a way toward it, and making tiny improvements along the way—to accomplish all of her other goals, including being a TV reporter and a commercial pilot![4]

If you want to achieve something, the key is to start moving in that direction. Give yourself permission to do so. Look around for holes in your organization, ask for what you want, find ways to leverage your skills and experiences, be willing to make the first move, and stretch beyond what you've done before. There are always opportunities waiting to be exploited. Instead of waiting to be asked and tiptoeing around an opportunity, seize it. It takes hard work, energy, and drive—but these are the assets that set leaders apart from those who wait for others to anoint them.

Chapter 5

The Secret Sauce of
Silicon Valley

I require my students to write a failure résumé. That is, to craft a résumé that summarizes all their biggest screwups—personal, professional, and academic. For every failure, each student must describe what he or she learned from that experience. Imagine the looks of surprise this assignment inspires in students who are so used to showcasing their successes. However, after they finish their résumé, they realize that this assignment has forced them to come to terms with their mistakes and to extract lessons from those experiences. As the years go by, many former students continue to keep their failure résumé up to date, in parallel with their traditional résumé of successes.

I borrowed this assignment from Liz Kisenwether at Penn State University. When I first heard the idea I thought it was terrific. It's a quick way to demonstrate that failure is an important part of your learning process, especially when you're stretching your abilities, doing things for the first time, or taking risks. People who have experience are hired not just because of their successes but also because of their failures. Failures offer learning opportunities and increase the chance that you won't make the same mistake again. Failures are also a sign that you have taken on challenges that expand your skills. In fact, if you aren't failing sometimes, then you aren't taking enough risks.

I showed an early version of this book's manuscript to some students, and several urged me to include a sample failure résumé. I realized that it had to be mine. So, here is my own abbreviated failure résumé, showcasing some of my biggest mistakes. I wish I had kept this résumé up to date for the past forty years. It would have been fascinating to revisit and learn from all the mistakes I've conveniently put out of my mind.

TINA L. SEELIG

PROFESSIONAL FAILURES

NOT PAYING ATTENTION: Early in my career I naively thought I knew how organizations worked. I made judgments about corporate culture that were incorrect. I wish I had spent more time paying attention and less time making assumptions.

QUITTING TOO EARLY: While running my own business, I hit a wall. It got incredibly hard both technically and organizationally, and it was going to take a tremendous amount of effort to find my way to a solution. I wish I had been confident enough to fully commit to finding a solution instead of selling the company way too early.

ACADEMIC FAILURES

NOT DOING MY BEST: The first two years of college I didn't put my focused effort into all my courses. I missed the chance to extract the most value from the classes—a chance I can't get back.

MISMANAGING RELATIONSHIPS: I had a challenging relationship with my PhD advisor. I wanted to spend a lot of time teaching, and she felt I should spend most of my time in the lab. I wish I had found a way to better align our goals.

PERSONAL FAILURES

AVOIDING CONFLICTS: I had a boyfriend in college, and as we closed in on graduation, we were both stressed about where we were going next. Instead of dealing with the questions about our future directly, I blew up the relationship. I wish I had been able to talk honestly about what was going on.

NOT LISTENING TO MY GUT: My uncle died in New York. I lived in California, and several people in my family urged me not to travel to the funeral since it might inconvenience them. I have always regretted it. I learned that there are some things you can't undo. In this situation I could have let others know that I would manage my own travel arrangements to reduce the burden on others.

Recently, Johannes Haushofer, a prominent psychology and public affairs professor at Princeton, crafted his failure résumé to show his students that the path to success is filled with missteps and disappointments. He eventually put it online to share with a wider audience. The document details all the jobs he didn't get, rejection letters for research papers, and funding that fell through over several decades. What is his biggest failure? That his failure résumé ended up getting more attention than his entire body of academic work![1]

•   •   •

Willingness to take risks and reactions to failure differ dramatically around the world. In some cultures the downside for failure is so high that individuals are allergic to taking any risks at all. These cultures associate shame with any type of failure, and from a young age people are taught to follow a prescribed path with a well-defined chance of success, as opposed to trying anything that might lead to disappointment. In some places, such as Thailand, someone who has failed repeatedly might even choose to take on a brand-new name in an attempt to reboot his or her entire life. In fact, in the 2008 Olympics, a Thai weight lifter attributed her victory to changing her name before the games.

The Global Entrepreneurship Monitor (GEM),[2] which publishes a detailed annual report on startup activity around the world, looks at cultural differences in risk-taking and comfort with failure. The GEM team has found that important factors contribute to a society's risk profile. For example, in some countries, such as Sweden, the bankruptcy laws are designed such that once your company goes out of business you can never get out of debt. Knowing that failure has drastic, long-term consequences for you and your family is a huge disincentive to try to start a company in the first place. The culture in other countries is equally unforgiving. In some parts of the world, once you fail, your friends, neighbors, and colleagues will always view you as a failure. An article in the *Wall Street Journal* describes humiliating tactics used by debt collectors in several countries, including Spain.[3] The collectors literally show up at individuals' houses in bizarre costumes, with the goal of drawing attention from the neighbors and shaming the debtors. Why would anyone in these communities risk public ridicule by taking on any unnecessary risk?

Bob Eberhart, a professor of organization theory and entrepreneurship, did research on how the changing bankruptcy laws in Japan affect the amount of entrepreneurial activity in that country. This was a natural experiment that could be studied because Japan removed the most difficult consequences of company failure in an attempt to revive the country's economy. The results showed that after the cost of failure was lowered, more people founded high-potential companies than when the consequences for failure were high.[4]

Silicon Valley is known as a place where failure is acknowledged as a natural part of the innovation process, and accepting failures on the way to success is considered the secret sauce of Silicon Valley. Randy Komisar notes that being able to view failure as an asset is the hallmark of an entrepreneurial environment. He also notes that when he sees people who never admit to failures, he wonders what they have really learned from their experiences.

Of course, nobody wants to fail. However, on the most basic level, all learning comes from failure. Think of a baby learning to walk. He or she starts out crawling and then falling before finally mastering the skill that as an adult most of us take for granted. As a child gets older, each new feat, from catching a baseball to doing algebra, is learned the same way, by experimenting and failing until that child is finally successful. We don't expect a child to do everything perfectly the first time; nor should we expect adults who take on complex tasks to get it all right the first time.

It is nearly impossible to learn anything without doing it yourself and failing until you succeed. You can't learn to play soccer by reading a rulebook, you can't learn to play the piano by studying sheets of music, and you can't learn to cook by reading recipes. I'm reminded of my time as a graduate student in neuroscience. I had taken several courses in which we "learned" the principles of neurophysiology. Although I could pass a written test on the material, it wasn't until I was in a lab, dissecting nerves under a microscope, impaling them with tiny electrodes, and manually turning the dials on the oscilloscope, that I fully understood the concepts with trial-and-error experiments. Likewise, you can read as many books on leadership as you want, but until you experience the challenges real leaders face, you will not be prepared to take charge.

The Mayfield Fellows Program, which I have codirected with Tom Byers for nearly twenty years, gives students this opportunity.[5] After one quarter of classroom work, during which we offer an in-depth introduction to entrepreneurship through case studies, the twelve students in this nine-month program spend the summer working in startup companies.

They take on key roles in each business and are closely mentored by senior leaders in the company. They experience firsthand what it is like to identify and address the white-hot risks that face each organization, the stresses of making decisions with incomplete information, and the challenge of leading in an ever-changing environment. After the intense summer experience, the students come back to class for ten weeks of debriefing about what happened in their respective companies. Each student leads a class on an important issue that evolved during their internship.

The students in the Mayfield Fellows Program develop powerful insights about what it means to run a fast-paced business in a dynamic environment. They watch these companies struggle with issues such as running out of cash, retooling after a change in the senior management team, the challenge of getting cutting-edge technology to work, and the daunting task of competing against giants in the industry. By the end of the summer, the students realize that only a handful of the companies for which they worked will be in business in a few years. Despite all of the efforts of talented teams, many of them will fail.

The entire venture-capital industry essentially invests in failures, since the majority of the companies they fund eventually go under. Other industries have a similar success rate, including the toy industry, the movie business, and the publishing industry. Consider book publishing. There are approximately one million books published every year in the United States, and about half of those are self-published. According to BookScan, the average US book sells fewer than 250 copies per year and less than 3,000 copies over its lifetime.[6] Only a tiny fraction will be big hits, and it's nearly impossible to predict which ones they will be. As a result, publishers continue to produce many different books, hoping that each will be a success but knowing that only a tiny fraction will make it onto a bestsellers list. Publishers, toy makers, movie producers, and venture capitalists understand that the path to success is littered with failures.

Mir Imran, a serial entrepreneur, has started dozens of companies, many in parallel.[7] His success rate has been remarkable. When asked about this, Mir admits that the key is killing projects early. He uses a brutal process to weed out projects with a low likelihood of success and puts increased energy into those with a high likelihood of making it to the finish line. He uses considerable discipline and analysis in the early stages, prior to launching a new venture, to increase the chances that it will thrive in the long run.

•   •   •

Even though it is always difficult to abandon a project, it is much easier to do so in the early stages of a venture, before there is an enormous escalation of committed time and energy. This happens in all parts of our lives, including jobs, stock investments, and any type of relationship. Leonardo da Vinci is credited with saying, "It is easier to resist at the beginning than at the end." Bob Sutton, an expert on organizational behavior, describes "The da Vinci Rule" in his book *The No Asshole Rule*, in which he talks about leaving jobs that are not a good match as soon as you discover they are untenable. Here he generalizes this much more broadly:

Although most people know that sunk costs shouldn't be considered in making a decision, the "too-much-invested-to-quit syndrome" is a powerful driver of human behavior. We justify all the time, effort, suffering, and years and years that we devote to something by telling ourselves and others that there must be something worthwhile and important about it or we never would have sunk so much of our lives into it.[8]

Quitting is actually incredibly empowering. It's a reminder that you control the situation and can leave whenever you like. You don't have to be your own prison guard, keeping yourself locked up in a place that isn't working. But that doesn't mean quitting is easy. I've quit jobs that were a bad match and abandoned failing projects, and in each case it was terribly difficult. We're taught that quitting is a sign of weakness, although in many circumstances it's just the opposite. Sometimes quitting is the bravest alternative, because it requires you to face the fact that things are not working. The great news is that quitting allows you to start over with a clean slate. And if you take the time to evaluate what happened, quitting can be an invaluable learning experience.

When Randy Komisar left his vice president position at Claris, a computer software company that spun out of Apple Computer, he felt he had failed. He had a clear vision of what he wanted to accomplish and left Claris when he realized he was never going to achieve his goals. Randy's "failure" was very public, and it stung badly. However, within a short time Randy realized that being released from this job provided him with an opportunity to reevaluate his passions and determine how he could best use his skills. For instance, it became clear that one reason he felt so dissatisfied at Claris was that he was neither passionate about the product nor passionate about what he was doing. He loved thinking about the company's big picture and scoping out its vision, but he was hardly inspired by the day-to-day management issues.

When Randy was asked to become CEO of a new company, he suggested instead that he work *with* the CEO to set the direction for the company. In this way he crafted a brand-new role for himself—virtual CEO—and was subsequently able to become involved with dozens of companies, many at the same time. He served as a coach, sounding board, and advisor for CEOs but didn't have the day-to-day responsibilities. This suited him and the companies well. Randy told me the failure allowed him to better align his passions with the opportunities around him. This is a poignant reminder that learning when to call it quits is crucial. You need to know when to stop pounding on an idea that isn't working and when to move on to something new.

There are actually many ways to turn a failure into a success. One memorable story about transforming a big disappointment into a big win came out of the Innovation Tournament in which students had to create value from rubber bands in five days. One team decided to create a Wishing Tree. They identified a tree in the center of campus, across from the university bookstore and wrapped the trunk with chicken wire. They then used rubber bands to attach messages to the chicken wire. The idea was that anyone passing by could post a wish on the tree. The team promoted it widely, using online networking sites and email lists, and by literally standing in front of the tree, inviting passersby to post a wish. Unfortunately, people just weren't interested.

In an attempt to build momentum, the team started seeding the tree with wishes. This had little effect. They then became more aggressive in their promotion and more actively invited passersby to contribute. Again, this had little impact. But the students' disappointment was amplified by the fact that not more than fifty feet away a similar project was getting lots of attention. Another team had created a huge web of large rubber bands from which they invited students to suspend their secrets. The rubber-band web was brimming with hundreds of brightly colored papers, each with a different secret. They fluttered in the light breeze, in sharp contrast to the nearly naked Wishing Tree next door.

The Wishing Tree team decided to chalk this one up as a failure. However, they didn't stop there. They extracted as much as they could from this experience by making a provocative three-minute video documenting the failure. The team described all of their attempts to make the Wishing Tree successful and compared their failure to the success of the Web of Secrets. They very publicly celebrated their failure and shared what they had learned about the "stickiness" of wishes versus secrets. Stories, products, and websites are "sticky" when they hold your attention and don't let go. The team also made it clear that this was just one step along the path to the next idea, and the next, and the next. They clearly learned something about the innovation process since they went on to win the Stanford business plan competition later that year for their medical technology venture.[9]

Because even great ideas require a tremendous amount of work to reach a successful outcome, it's incredibly hard to know when to keep pushing on a problem, hoping for a break-through, and when to walk away. We all know that persistence is to be admired, but when does it become foolish to continue working on something that's never going to fly? Gil Penchina, a serial entrepreneur and venture capitalist, describes the di-lemma wonderfully: "If you throw gasoline on a log, all you get is a wet log. But if you throw gasoline on a small flame, you get an inferno."[10] That is, it's important to know whether you're putting energy into something that has the potential to pay off. This is one of life's biggest challenges. We often stay in dead-end situations way too long. This occurs when compa-nies commit to a doomed product or project, or when individu-als stay with jobs or in relationships that make them miserable, hoping the situation will improve.

Yes, failure is hard. But it is a normal part of the learning process. Instead of looking at false starts and dead ends with regret, I suggest that you look at each one as a source of "data." Scientists do this all the time. They know that each experi-ment may lead to unexpected results. And the unexpected re-sults are often a source of great inspiration. This is true in all parts of life. If you view each day as a series of experiments, you end up with lots of fascinating data that can be mined for valuable insights.

Chapter 6

Turbulence Ahead

How do you know when to quit and when to push through a problem? It's always a mammoth challenge to separate your desire to make something work from the probability that it will or won't. Of course, the more you put into a project, the more likely it is to succeed. But some efforts will never pan out, no matter how much time, money, or sweat is invested. The most scientific answer I've found is to listen to your gut and look at your alternatives. Essentially, you have to negotiate honestly with yourself. Do you have the fortitude to push through the problems in front of you to reach a successful outcome, or are you better off taking another path?

If you decide to quit, make sure that you do it well. That is easier said than done. I've seen people quit gracefully and others quit so clumsily that they leave a huge crater in their wake. As discussed earlier, you are likely to bump into the same people again and again in life, often in unexpected ways. This alone is reason enough to make sure that when you quit, you do so with careful thought about the consequences for those around you. Besides the impact that quitting gracefully might have on you later, it is just the right thing to do. You can never rationalize quitting in such a way that you hurt your colleagues, friends, or former business.

A colleague told me about his assistant, who was doing a terrific job. He gave her great reviews and spent a lot of time talking with her about her career path within his group. She made it clear that ultimately she hoped to move into a different field, and my colleague was supportive of this. In fact, he told her he would be delighted to serve as a reference for her anytime. With this as a backdrop, my colleague couldn't have been more surprised when his assistant came in one day and gave two weeks' notice. The team was in the midst of a huge project, the deadline three weeks away. She was going to leave one week before the project was completed, putting the entire team in a very difficult position. My colleague asked her several times if she would consider staying one more week to help him get to the end of the project, which involved dozens of people directly and several thousand indirectly. She refused, saying, "I know you're going to be unhappy that I'm leaving no matter when I go, so I decided to do what I want." My colleague felt as though he'd been kicked in the stomach. It was nearly impossible to fill in the holes she left during the last week of the project, and everyone worked around the clock to try to fill the void. All those who worked with her will remember that decision. Despite the fact that she did a great job while she was with them, the damage she did to her reputation during the last weeks of her employment dwarfed all the positive things she had done in prior years.

In sharp contrast, I've seen others quit jobs with remarkable style. Even if they were leaving because the job wasn't a good match, the way in which they left made such a positive impression that everyone involved would be pleased to give them a glowing recommendation at any time in the future. They provided enough notice to fill any gaps, they took the time to put their work in order so someone else could pick up where they had left off, and they even offered to help with the transition. They mastered the art of quitting with grace.

• • •

Instead of quitting, there is often a huge bonus for working through a tough situation. Sometimes this involves figuring out how to collaborate with a challenging person, how to succeed with limited resources, or how to fix an unexpected technical problem. A great example is Debbie Sterling, the founder of GoldieBlox, which makes construction toys for girls to help them learn engineering. She was inspired to launch this company based on her own lack of exposure as a girl to the power of engineering to solve important problems in the world. After spending countless hours scaling the scrappy startup, beginning with a very successful Kickstarter campaign, she and her small team finally reached escape velocity by raising a million dollars to help them develop the product.

Then, using grassroots marketing, they won the right to air a commercial during the 2014 Super Bowl, which resulted in huge exposure and enthusiasm. Orders for the GoldieBlox products began pouring in, and they started shipping tens of thousands of units of their toys. Unfortunately, things did not go smoothly, and scaling so fast came at a price. The physical blocks in the product turned out to have a problem—they didn't fit together properly. The company received complaints from customers, telling them the toy was flawed. This was a devastating blow to Debbie and her team. After so much work and success, they were hit with this huge failure. What to do?

They decided to take apart the problem and solve it as an engineer would do. After dealing with the manufacturing issues and fixing the blocks, they needed to rebuild trust with their disappointed customers. They did this by literally sending a million new blocks to all of their customers, explaining the mistakes they had made and how they had fixed them. Most important, they wrote a personalized letter to each child from the fictional character in the game, Goldie, explaining that engineers don't always get it right the first time, but that doesn't mean that you should give up. They explained what had happened and shared the engineering drawings of the old and new blocks. This negative experience turned into a positive learning opportunity for the business and for their customers. In fact, they turned this failure into a powerful opportunity to gain more trust and support for the company and the product.[1]

This example demonstrates how this dance works. Debbie had to change her own emotional response from deep disappointment to optimism, she had to change the conversation with her customers from one of frustration to one of appreciation, and she had to change her relationship with the overall problem by seeing it as an opportunity.

This theme comes up again and again when listening to those who have been successful, whether they have faced big or small challenges. They are willing to try lots of things and are confident that some of their experiments will lead to great outcomes. But they also recognize that there will be potholes along the way. This approach can be used for big and small challenges. The following story was told to me by a friend: There was a man who appeared to have endless luck with women. He wasn't particularly charming, funny, smart, or attractive, so it was quite a mystery. One day my friend asked him how he managed to have such a steady flow of women in his life. He confided that it was simple—he asked every attractive woman he met for a date, and some of them said yes. He was willing to take his share of rejections in return for a handful of successes. This brings the lesson to its basest level. If you get out there and try lots of things, you're much more likely to find success than someone who waits around for the phone to ring.

This story is consistent with advice my father always gave me: being a squeaky wheel rarely changes the outcome, but it does allow you to get to the conclusion sooner. Don't sit around waiting for a yes that will never come. It's better to get to no sooner rather than later so you can put your energy into opportunities with a higher likelihood of success. This applies to job hunting, finding business funding, dating, and most other endeavors. That is, if you continue to push the limits and are willing to fail along the way, you will very likely find success. As described by Alberto Savoia in *The Right It*, this type of experimentation is called "pretotyping."[2] It involves performing quick experiments to rapidly determine if you are going in the right direction so you can continue adding fuel to the fire if the experiments prove you are onto something or abandon the effort if you are going in the wrong direction.

Unrealistically, many people feel as though they should be consistently progressing up and to the right, moving along a straight success line. But this never happens, and is actually limiting. When you look closely at a graph representing a successful person's career, there are always ups and downs. When viewed over a longer time period, however, the line moves up and to the right. When you are in a down cycle it is hard to see that the temporary dip is actually a setup for the next rise. In fact, the slope of the upward line is often steeper after a down cycle, meaning you are really achieving more than if you had stayed on a steady, predictable upward path.

Carol Bartz, the former CEO of Autodesk and Yahoo!, uses another great analogy to describe a successful career path.[3] She thinks you should look at the progress of your career as moving around and up a three-dimensional pyramid, as opposed to up a two-dimensional ladder. Lateral moves along the side of the pyramid often allow you to build the base of your experience. It may not look as though you're moving up quickly, but you're gathering a foundation of skills and experiences that will prove extremely valuable later.

Adding another perspective, Josh McFarland, who has been deeply embedded in the world of startups for twenty years, points out that we are more sensitive to the rate of change in our position than the actual position. He says, "We actually feel acutely the rate of change more than the absolute value at any one point in time. . . . Think about when you're flying in a plane. You can't really tell if you're going 300 or 400 miles an hour. You can tell, however, when you're accelerating and decelerating. . . . [Also,] it's really hard to tell whether you're at

30,000 feet or 35,000 feet, [but] you can really tell when you hit a pocket of turbulence and you drop 500 feet. . . . So, when things are getting better, it feels really great. When things are getting worse, it feels really bad, regardless of where you are on that continuum of being up and to the right."[4]

A classic story about the cyclical and unpredictable nature of careers comes from Steve Jobs. As the founder of Apple and Pixar, his success stories are legendary. However, many of his finest successes grew out of failures. He described these stories beautifully when he gave the commencement address at Stanford in 2005. Here is an excerpt of his speech:

> We had just released our finest creation—the Macintosh—a year earlier, and I had just turned thirty. And then I got fired. How can you get fired from a company you started? Well, as Apple grew we hired someone who I thought was very talented to run the company with me, and for the first year or so things went well. But then our visions of the future began to diverge, and eventually we had a falling out. When we did, our board of directors sided with him. So at thirty I was out. And very publicly out. What had been the focus of my entire adult life was gone, and it was devastating.
>
> I really didn't know what to do for a few months. I felt that I had let the previous generation of entrepreneurs down—that I had dropped the baton as it was being passed to me. I met with David Packard and Bob Noyce and tried to apologize for screwing up so badly.

I was a very public failure, and I even thought about running away from the valley. But something slowly began to dawn on me: I still loved what I did. The turn of events at Apple had not changed that one bit. I had been rejected, but I was still in love. And so I decided to start over.

I didn't see it then, but it turned out that getting fired from Apple was the best thing that could have ever happened to me. The heaviness of being successful was replaced by the lightness of being a beginner again, less sure about everything. It freed me to enter one of the most creative periods of my life. During the next five years, I started a company named NeXT, another company named Pixar, and fell in love with an amazing woman who would become my wife. Pixar went on to create the world's first computer-animated feature film, *Toy Story*, and is now the most successful animation studio in the world. In a remarkable turn of events, Apple bought NeXT, I returned to Apple, and the technology we developed at NeXT is at the heart of Apple's current renaissance. And Laurene and I have a wonderful family together.

I'm pretty sure none of this would have happened if I hadn't been fired from Apple. It was awful-tasting medicine, but I guess the patient needed it. Sometimes life hits you in the head with a brick.[5]

This story is echoed time and time again. Essentially, most individuals' paths are riddled with small and enormous failures.

The key is being able to recover from them. One of my favorite sayings is "It's all good in the end. If it's not good, it's not the end." We are always in the middle of the story, and there is usually a way to recover.

• • •

For most successful people, the bottom is lined with rubber as opposed to concrete. When they hit bottom, they sink in for a bit and then bounce back, tapping into the energy of the impact to propel them into another opportunity. A great example is David Neeleman, the founder of JetBlue.[6] David initially started an airline called Morris Air, which grew and prospered, and he sold it to Southwest Airlines for $130 million in 1993. He then became an employee of Southwest.

After only five months, David was fired. He was miserable working for Southwest, and as he says, he was driving them crazy. As part of his contract, he had a five-year non-compete agreement that prevented him from starting another airline. That seemed like a lifetime to wait. But after taking time to recover from this blow, David decided to spend that time planning for his next airline venture. He thought through all the details of the company, including the corporate values, the complete customer experience, the type of people they would hire, as well as how they would train and compensate their employees. David says that getting fired and having to wait to start another airline was the best thing that ever happened to him. When the non-compete period was over, he was ready to hit the ground running and launched JetBlue. Just like Steve

Jobs, he was able to turn what seemed like a terrible situation into a period of extreme productivity and creativity.

Failing, of course, isn't fun. It's much more fun to tell the world about our successes. But failures can serve as incredible opportunities in disguise. They force us to reevaluate our goals and priorities, and often propel us forward much faster than continued success.

Getting too comfortable with failure, however, seems risky. Are those who celebrate failure doomed to fail? Imagine corporate Employee of the Month photos showcasing the biggest screwups. However, as Bob Sutton points out in *Weird Ideas That Work*, rewarding only successes can stifle innovation because it discourages risk-taking. Bob suggests that organizations consider rewarding successes *and* failures, and punishing inaction. Doing so would encourage people to experiment, which is more likely to lead to interesting and unexpected outcomes.

> I am not saying that your company should reward people who are stupid, lazy, or incompetent. I mean you should reward smart failures, not dumb failures. If you want a creative organization, inaction is the worst kind of failure. . . . Creativity results from action, rather than inaction, more than anything else.[7]

Bob adds that there is strong evidence that the ratio between our individual successes and failures stays the same. Therefore, if you want more successes, you're going to have to be willing to live with more failures. Failure is the flip side of success, and you can't have one without the other.

At the d.school there is a lot of emphasis on taking big risks to earn big rewards. Students are encouraged to think really *big*, even if there's a significant chance that a project won't be successful. To encourage this, we reward spectacular disasters. Students are told that it is much better to have a flaming failure than a so-so success. Jim Plummer, the former dean of Stanford's School of Engineering, embraces this philosophy. He tells his PhD students that they should pick a thesis project that has a 20 percent chance of success. Some students find this discouraging, interpreting this to mean they will have to do five different projects before they reach completion. Quite the contrary. The experiments should be designed so that a failure is informative and a success leads to a major breakthrough. Doing small, incremental experiments with predictable results is much less valuable than taking a big risk that will potentially lead to a much bigger reward.

We often live on the edge of success and failure, and it is rarely clear which way we will land. This uncertainty is amplified in high-risk ventures, such as restaurants, technology startups, and even sports, where the line between success and failure may be razor thin. Consider the Tour de France. Even after twenty-one days of cycling up and down steep and winding mountain roads, the time difference between the winners and the losers boils down to a matter of minutes. Sometimes a little extra push is all it takes to flip the switch from failure to success.

Some companies have mastered the ability to coax the value from products that others might discard as failures. Google and other web-based companies rely upon A-B testing. That is, they release two or more versions of software at the same time and receive quick feedback on what approach is more successful.

These companies find that by making small modifications, such as changing the color of a button, adding a single word to a message, or moving images around on a page, they change the customers' experience and that can dramatically alter their feedback. Some businesses release dozens of versions of the same software product a day, each altering the user experience in some small way so the businesses can evaluate the responses.

• • •

Trying new things requires a willingness to take risks. However, risk-taking is not binary. Most people are comfortable taking some types of risks and find other types quite uncomfortable. You might not even see in advance which risks are comfortable for you to take, discounting their riskiness, but you are likely to amplify the risk of things that make you more anxious. For example, you might love flying down a ski slope at lightning speed or jumping out of airplanes and don't view these activities as risky. If so, you're blind to the fact that you're taking on significant physical risk. Others, who are not physical risk-takers, would rather sip hot chocolate in the ski lodge or buckle themselves tightly into their airplane seats than strap on a pair of ski boots or a parachute. Alternately, you might feel perfectly comfortable with social risks, such as giving a speech to a large crowd. But others, who might be perfectly happy jumping out of a plane, would never speak in a public forum.

There are many types of risks, including physical, social, emotional, financial, ethical, creative, political, and intellectual. I ask my students to map their own risk profile using this Risk-o-Meter.

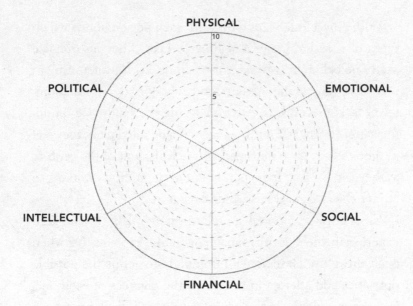

Here is an example of my own:

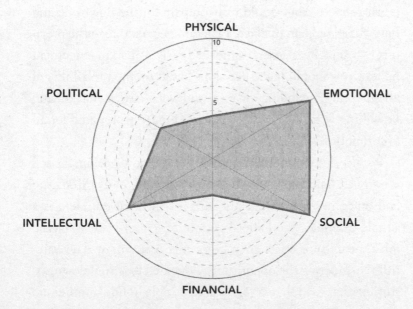

With only a little bit of reflection, each person knows which types of risks he or she is willing to take. They also realize pretty quickly that risk-taking isn't uniform. It's interesting to note that most entrepreneurs and investors don't see themselves as big risk-takers. After analyzing the landscape, building a great team, and putting together a detailed plan, they feel as though they have squeezed as much risk out of the venture as they can. In fact, they spend most of their efforts working to reduce the risks, or de-risk, their businesses.

Elisabeth Paté-Cornell, a professor in our department, is an expert in the field of risk management. She explains that when analyzing a risky situation, it's important to define the possible outcomes and attempt to figure out the chances of each one. Once this is done, one needs to develop a full plan for each eventuality. Elisabeth says it makes sense to take the high risk/ high reward path if you're willing to live with all the potential consequences. You should fully prepare for the downside and have a backup plan in place. I encourage you to read the previous two sentences several times. Experts in risk management believe you should make decisions based on the probability of all outcomes, including the best- and worst-case scenarios, and be willing to take big risks when you are fully prepared for all eventualities.

It's also important to remember that good decisions, based on an accurate analysis of the risks involved, can still lead to bad outcomes. That's because risk is still involved. Here is a simple example. Soon after I got out of school I was offered a job I wasn't sure was a great fit for me. After many days carefully considering the opportunity, I decided to turn it down, assuming that soon thereafter I would be able to find another job that was a better match. Unfortunately, the economy turned south quite quickly, and I spent months looking for another job. I kicked myself for not taking that position, which started to look more and more appealing. I had made a good decision, based on all the information I had at the time, but in the short run it wasn't a great outcome. This happens frequently since we aren't in control of all the variables.

As in this situation, under most circumstances you have to make decisions with incomplete information. That is, you have to make a choice and take action in the face of consider-able uncertainty surrounding each option. So, how do you fill in the gaps of your knowledge? I suggest looking to "Stanley" for inspiration. The inner workings of Stanley, the autonomous vehicle designed and built by Stanford's Artificial Intelligence Laboratory and Volkswagen Electronics Research Laboratory for the DARPA Grand Challenge, offer clues to decision-making with incomplete information. DARPA, the Defense Advanced Research Projects Agency, is a government agency charged with the development of cutting-edge technology for the military. In the DARPA competition, driverless cars must navigate a 212-kilometer off-road race. Each must pass through three narrow tunnels, make more than a hundred sharp turns, and navigate mountain passes with steep cliffs on each side. Despite very low odds, Stanford's car won the race.

Stanley had a lot of powerful technology on board, includ-ing three-dimensional maps of the terrain, GPS, gyroscopes, accelerometers, video cameras, and sensors on the wheels. The on-board software analyzed and interpreted all incoming data and controlled the vehicle's speed and direction. But the key to Stanley's victory was its superior skill at making decisions with incomplete information. The designers accomplished this by building in the ability for it to learn the way humans do. They created a database of human decisions the car drew upon when making judgments about what to do. These data were incorporated into a learning program tied to the car's control systems and greatly reduced errors in judgment.

This story highlights the fact that learning from others can significantly reduce your failure rate. You don't have to figure everything out yourself. Like Stanley, you should gather all the data you can from your environment and then tap into the wisdom of those who have gone before you in order to make the best possible choice. All you need to do is look around to see hundreds, if not thousands, of role models for every choice you plan to make.

If you do take a risk and happen to fail, remember that you personally are not a failure. The failure is external. This perspective will allow you to get up and try again and again. Your idea might have been poor, the timing might have been off, or you might not have had the necessary resources to succeed. As Jeff Hawkins says, "You are not your company. You are not your product. It's real easy to believe you are, and it's real easy to get wrapped up in it. . . . If you fail, or even if you're successful, you really need to separate these things. . . . Your company may fail, your product may fail, but you're not going to be a failure."[8] Failure is a natural part of the learning process. If you aren't failing sometimes, then you probably aren't taking enough risks.

Chapter 7

No Way . . . Engineering Is for Girls

How many people have told you that the key to success is to follow your passion? I'd bet a lot. Giving that advice to someone who's struggling to figure out what to do with his or her life is easy. However, that advice is actually simplistic and misleading. Don't get me wrong, I'm a huge fan of passion and think it's incredibly important to know what drives you. But it certainly isn't enough.

Passion is just a starting point. You also need to know your talents and how the world values them. If you're passionate about something but not particularly good at it, then it's going to be pretty frustrating to try to craft a career in that area. Say you love basketball but aren't tall enough to compete, or you're enthralled by jazz but can't carry a tune. In both cases you can be a terrific *fan*, going to games and concerts, without being a professional.

Taking this a step further, perhaps you're passionate about something *and* are quite talented in the field, but there's no existing market for those skills. For example, you might be a skilled artist and love to paint, or crave surfing and can ride any wave. But we all know the market for these skills is small. Trying to craft a career around such a passion is often a recipe for frustration. You have two choices: you can think of it as a wonderful hobby and do it on the side, or if you are fully committed to building a career around it, then you will need to build an audience for your work. The latter is described in chapter 8, where Perry Klebahn builds a market for the snow-shoes he invented.

Alternately, if you have talent in an area and there's a big market for your skills, but you don't find the work satisfying, then that is a great area in which to find a *job*. For example, if you are an accomplished accountant, there's always a position for someone who can build a balance sheet. For most people in the world, this is where they live. They have a job that uses their skills, but they can't wait to get home to focus on the ac-tivities they love—their hobbies. They count the days until the weekend, until vacation, or until retirement. The worst-case scenario is finding yourself in a position where you have no passion for your work and no skills in the field and there's no market for what you're doing. Take the classic joke about trying to sell snow to Eskimos. Now imagine doing that if you hate snow and are a terrible salesperson. It's a bad situation all the way around.

The sweet spot is where your passion overlaps with your skills and the market. If you can find that spot, then you're in the wonderful position in which your job enriches your life instead of just providing the financial resources that allow you to enjoy your life *after* the workday is over. The goal should be a *career* in which you can't believe people actually pay you to do your job.

A quote often attributed to the Chinese Taoist philosopher Lao-tzu sums this up:

> The master of the art of living makes little distinction between his work and his play, his labor and his leisure, his mind and his body, his education and his recreation, his love and his religion. He simply pursues his vision of excellence in whatever he does, leaving others to decide whether he is working or playing. To him, he is always doing both.

The wisdom of this is reflected in the observation that hard work plays a huge part in making you successful. And the truth is, we simply tend to work harder at things we're passionate about. This is easy to see in children who spend hours working at the things they love to do. A child passionate about building will spend hours designing amazing structures with blocks. A child who loves art will draw for hours without a break. And to a child who loves sports, shooting hoops or hitting baseballs all afternoon will seem like fun, not practice. Passion is a big driver. It makes each of us want to work hard to perfect our skills and to excel.

It is important to understand, though, that most of us aren't born with specific passions, but they grow from our experiences. Before something is your passion, it is something you know nothing about. You would have no idea that you were good at cooking and really enjoyed it until you tried it. The same is true with software coding, playing golf, and writing novels. Engaging in new activities is critically important because it opens the door to developing—not finding—a wide variety of passions. Mike Rowe, famous for his *Dirty Jobs* television show in which he took on tasks that got him far outside his comfort zone, says it beautifully: "Never follow your passion, but always bring it with you."[1]

The process of finding the gold mine where your skills, your interests, and the market overlap can take some time. Consider Nathan Furr, who started his academic career as an English major and dreamed of being a professor. Like many English majors, Nathan soon realized that the market for English professors was impossibly limited. And even if he got a job in the field, the compensation would be pretty low. This was going to be a tough way to support the big family he was planning. Nathan spent some time thinking about other ways he could use his skills and channel his passions. After scanning the horizon for other options, it became pretty clear that he would fit well in the world of management consulting, which would allow him to use his research and writing skills, as well as his joy of learning. The only problem was that Nathan didn't know enough to get that first job in the field. So he gave himself a year to prepare. He joined organizations on his college campus that would allow him to learn more about consulting, and he practiced doing mini case studies, such as those presented during a typical job interview. By the time the one-year mark rolled around, Nathan was ready and landed a prime job as a management consultant for a top firm. It was a great fit in so many ways, tapping into his skills and his passions and providing him with the financial security he needed. Years later, he decided to build upon these interests by earning a PhD in management science and engineering, and is now a business professor at INSEAD in France. So, he started with a dream of being a professor and ultimately got there by finding ways to bridge his skills, his interests, and the market.

I share this story because it is relevant to all of us. If Nathan knew what he would be doing professionally when he was thirty-five, he would have been both surprised and delighted. But he would have had no idea how he was going to get from his starting point as an English major in Utah to a leading business school professor in France. The key is that by setting your intention on larger and larger goals, and taking a series of small steps in those directions, you ultimately achieve more than you could ever have imagined.

Nathan picked a career path after he'd been exposed to a variety of options. But most of us are encouraged to plan much further ahead. People love to ask kids, "What do you want to be when you grow up?" This forces children to nail down their goals, at least in their minds, long before they've been exposed to the wide array of opportunities. We also typically visualize ourselves doing the things we see others doing in our immediate environment, which is a terribly limited view considering the world of possibilities. Also, my guess is that you, like me, were heavily influenced by people around you who liked to tell you what *they* thought you should be doing. I clearly remember one of my teachers saying, "You're really good at science. You should consider being a nurse." A fine suggestion, but it is only one of an almost infinite number of things one can do with a gift for science.

It is remarkable how one statement, often from a stranger, can shift the way one sees oneself and one's prospects. During my creativity course, teams of students each pick an organization they think is innovative. These teams visit the firm, interview employees, watch them in action, and come to their own conclusions about what makes the organization creative. They then present this information to the class in an innovative way. One team picked the San Jose Children's Discovery Museum. They followed the staff and visitors for days to see what really made it tick. At one station kids were building a miniature roller coaster, changing different variables to see the results, and an eight-year-old girl was experimenting with the equipment. She changed the length, the height, and the angles of the various parts and ran different simulations to see the effect. A member of the museum staff watched her experiment for a while and simply commented, "You're doing the same types of things that engineers do." Later that day my students asked the girl what she had learned at the museum. She thought for a second and said with confidence, "I learned that I could be an engineer."

Like the girl in the museum, we all receive explicit and implicit messages about the roles we're expected to play. A couple of years ago a colleague of mine, a mechanical engineering professor, told a remarkable story. She has several women friends from her university who are also engineers in different disciplines. They often come over to her house for dinner and socializing. When her son was young, he was usually around, watching and listening to their conversations. As he got older and proved to be good at math and science, someone said to him, "Gee, you should consider studying engineering." He twisted his face and said, "No way. Engineering is for girls." My women friends who are physicians have told me similar stories. Their young sons called discussions about medicine "girl talk."

We are all subject to these types of preconceptions. Consider the following riddle. A boy and his father are in an accident and end up in the hospital. The surgeon says, "I can't operate on this boy. He's my son." What's going on? When I told my very progressive women doctor friends this riddle, even they couldn't figure out that the surgeon in the riddle was the boy's *mother*. They tried to come up with convoluted answers to the riddle, all involving a male doctor. Once they were told the answer they were terribly embarrassed that they, too, had fallen into this traditional trap.

When I think back on the messages I received, it's clear that specific individuals had a big impact—some were encouraging and others were not. When I was about fourteen years old we had a close family friend who was a neurosurgeon. I was fascinated by the brain and finally mustered the courage to ask him about his work. He thought it was "cute" and made a joke. I was disappointed and didn't ask again.

It wasn't until college that I found a professional in the field who explicitly encouraged me to pursue my interest in the brain. I was in my first neuroscience class during my sophomore year and the professor gave us an unusual assignment. He asked us to design a series of experiments to figure out what a specific part of the brain does. He told us that nobody knew its role and that it was our job to come up with a set of experiments to find out. When I got my paper back a week later a note written on the top said, "Tina, you think like a scientist." At that moment I *became* a scientist. I had just been waiting for someone to acknowledge my enthusiasm—and to give me permission to pursue my interests. We are all powerfully influenced by the messages around us. Some are direct, such as a teacher saying, "You should be a nurse," or "You think like a scientist." Others are embedded in our environment, such as years of seeing only female engineers or male surgeons.

•   •   •

When I was in my early twenties, it was surprisingly difficult for me to separate what I wanted for myself and what others wanted for me. I know this is true for many of my students as well. They tell me they're getting so much "guidance" from others that they have a tough time figuring out what they want to do. I remember clearly that I sometimes had the urge to quit or to avoid things that others strongly encouraged me to do, just so I would have the space to figure out what I wanted, independent of what they wanted for me. For example, I started graduate school at the University of Virginia right after I graduated from the University of Rochester. My parents were thrilled. They were so proud of me and were comforted that my path for the next few years was set.

But after only one semester of graduate school, I decided that I really needed to take a break from school after visiting a friend in Santa Cruz, California. It was a terribly difficult decision, but I knew in my gut that I needed to be a leaf in the wind for a while in order to understand what was the right path for me. The hardest part of the entire process was telling my parents I was taking a leave of absence from graduate school. My decision was extremely hard for them. I appreciated their endless support and encouragement, but it also made it difficult for me to truly know if being in school was the right decision for me or if I was doing it to make them happy. I drove across the country to Santa Cruz, California, with my cat, with no idea of what I was going to do next.

In retrospect, taking a break from school turned out to be a pivotal decision. My time in Santa Cruz was completely un-structured, and I was ready for any eventuality. It was exciting and scary. It was the first time I didn't have a specific assign-ment, a focused goal, or a clear plan. Although often stressful, it was the perfect way to figure out what I really wanted to do. I took odd jobs so I could support myself and spent a lot of time walking and thinking at the beach. After a while I started going to the University of California at Santa Cruz's biology library to keep up on neuroscience literature. At first it was monthly, then weekly, then daily.

After about six months in Santa Cruz, I was ready to get back into the lab, but not ready to go back to graduate school. With that objective, I tracked down a list of the neuroscience faculty at Stanford University, which was not far away, and wrote each one a letter. I told them about my background and asked if they had a research job for me. Over the next few weeks, I got letters back from all of them, but no one had an open position. How-ever, one faculty member passed my letter on, and I received a call from a professor in the anesthesia department. He asked if I would like to work in the operating room testing new medical equipment on high-risk patients. I jumped at the chance.

Within days I was at Stanford, getting up at the crack of dawn, wearing surgical scrubs, and monitoring patients. This experience was fascinating in a million unexpected ways. Once the project was over, I managed to negotiate a job as a research assistant in a neuroscience lab and eventually applied to transfer to graduate school at Stanford. The admissions committee made me jump through flaming hoops, but I was now extremely motivated and did everything they required. Eventually I was accepted. Honestly, that was the proudest moment of my life. And I was starting graduate school for myself, not for others.

I've taken many detours that might look to others like a waste of time. But this wasn't the case at all. Not only did the twists in my path give me a fresh perspective on my goals, they also gave me time to experiment with options that helped confirm what I wanted to do.

People often feel pressured to make decisions about their career path very early and then stick with them for decades. They want to be a "fire and forget" missile that zeroes in on a target and pursues it relentlessly. But this just isn't how things work most of the time. Most people change course many times before finding the best match for their skills and interests. This is similar to the process of developing a product or designing new software—it's important to keep experimenting, trying lots of things until you find out what works. Being too set on your path too early will likely lead you in the wrong direction. A reader of the earlier version of this book sent me a note with a beautiful analogy that captures the essence of this idea. He said that "too often people are concerned about getting on the train *at the right time,* as opposed to getting on *the right train.*"

I've met many students who literally show me a detailed map of what they plan to do for the next fifty years. Not only is this unrealistic, but it's sadly limiting. There are so many unexpected experiences ahead that it's best to keep your eyes open instead of blinding yourself to the serendipitous options that might present themselves. Planning a career should be like traveling in a foreign country. Even if you prepare carefully, have an itinerary and a place to stay at night, the most interesting experiences usually aren't planned. You might end up meeting a fascinating person who shows you places that aren't in the guidebook, or you might miss your train and end up spending the day exploring a small town you hadn't planned to visit. I guarantee that the things you're likely to remember from the journey are those that weren't on your original schedule. They will be the unexpected things that jumped into your path, surprising you along the way.

Here's the secret that few people tell you: there is no right decision. If your first role after school isn't a good match, try something new. And, if the next one doesn't fit, try something else. And, if that role sucks, quit! Continue doing this until you find something that is a great match . . . Rinse and repeat. Rinse and repeat. Rinse and repeat. This is similar to dating. It is very unlikely that you will fall in love and get married to the first person you date. The best chance to find a compatible match is to meet *lots* of people. The dating process is usually filled with false starts and disappointments, but you will never be successful unless you embrace the process of discovery and accept the uncertainty.

I literally changed careers — not just jobs — every two years after I graduated from school until I finally found a career that fit. I was forty-one years old! Most important, *none* of my prior experiences were a waste of time, even though they weren't perfect. Each added to my toolbox, providing a wealth of skills that I use every day. Most other people have a similar story, and their career path makes much more sense when viewed through the rearview mirror.

There is another secret that few people share. The uncertainty that we face when we leave school *never* evaporates. There is uncertainty at each turn of our lives—when we start a new job, launch a new company, begin a new relationship, have a child, or retire. Each of these decisions and actions opens the door to considerable uncertainty—and opportunity!

The opposite of *uncertainty* is *certainty*. Would you really want a detailed script for your life, knowing exactly what will happen next month, next year, and next decade? For most people the answer is no. At the core, uncertainty leads to choices. It leads to opportunities. It leads to surprises!

•   •   •

Most events in your life snap into focus when looked at in retrospect. When you look back on your career path the story makes perfect sense. The road ahead, however, is always fuzzy. It's easy to get frustrated by the lack of visibility ahead. You can, however, do things to increase the odds that great opportunities will come your way by working in organizations that provide access to a steady stream of new and interesting people and projects.

It's a mistake to try to manage your career too closely. Consider Teresa Briggs, who leads the entire western region for Deloitte, the consulting firm. She began her career in the audit practice of the company, and after eighteen years in that role reasonably assumed she would be there forever. However, she eventually found herself in an unpredictable situation. New laws required auditors to rotate on and off assignments with individual clients so a fresh set of auditors could ensure the

business was being managed legally. Teresa had been working with a very large client, and when she rotated off the team
there weren't other comparable opportunities. But she learned
that a new Deloitte group was forming that focused on mergers
and acquisitions. While mergers and acquisitions was not her
area of expertise, she was offered the opportunity to take a key
position. She found that her skills transferred beautifully. Even
though Teresa would not have planned this path herself, she
realized that her ability to build relationships with clients and
lead teams allowed her to excel in this new role.

After a short time, Teresa was transferred to the Deloitte national office in New York, where her leadership and management skills again allowed her to shine. Teresa was then asked
to head up the Silicon Valley practice for the firm, where she
had to learn new strategies and a brand-new vocabulary, this
time for high technology. None of Teresa's steps could have
been predicted, and yet by her excelling in an organization
that presented a continuous flow of new opportunities, many
exciting roles and challenges materialized.

It is also important to reassess your life and career relatively
frequently. This self-assessment process forces you to come
to terms with the fact that sometimes it's time to move on to
a new environment in order to excel. Most people don't assess their roles frequently enough and so stay in positions for
years longer than they should, settling for suboptimal situations. There isn't a magic number for the amount of time you
should stay in one role before evaluating whether it's right or
not. But it makes sense to think about how often you do so.
Some people reassess and readjust their lives daily or weekly,
constantly optimizing. Others wait years before noticing that

they've ended up far from where they had hoped to be. The more frequently you assess your situation, looking for ways to fix problems, the more likely you are to find yourself in a position where things are going well. Also, it's best to address small problems that crop up in your life early and often, as opposed to waiting for problems to get so big that they seem intractable. That can only happen when you pay attention and figure out what actually needs to change.

Some situations literally force you to reevaluate your life. For instance, once you decide to start a family, the entire game changes. You're suddenly faced with the need to figure out how to balance parenting with your profession. As everyone knows, caring for young children takes an enormous amount of time and focused energy. It's both physically and emotionally demanding, and incredibly time consuming. Children keep you on your toes, and their needs change dramatically as they get older. Each year brings a brand-new set of responsibilities and a fresh set of challenges. As a result, parenting provides an ever-changing opportunity to be creative and helps build skills that are extremely valuable in any setting. It exercises your ability to multitask and to make decisions under pressure, and it certainly helps you master the art of negotiation.

Women especially face the daunting puzzle of figuring out how to fit together career and family obligations. From my experience, this challenge really is a great opportunity in disguise. Instead of considering traditional jobs that have limited flexibility, being a parent forces you to be innovative. Additionally, as your children's needs change, you can experiment with different jobs with different responsibilities. Although it is hard to see up close, one's career is long, and children are small for only a few years, allowing you to accelerate your career as your children grow up. The following excerpt from a 1997 edition of *Stanford Magazine* snaps this idea into focus.

> A 1950 [Stanford] graduate earned her law degree here in '52 and took five years out of the paid workforce after her second son was born, keeping herself busy and visible in volunteer work for the Phoenix Junior League and the Salvation Army. Later, when her youngest went off to school, she went back to work part-time in the state attorney general's office.
>
> Staying home with her children during those years ultimately didn't hamper her career. . . . She added that today's young graduates could fare even better than she did. "One help is that nowadays women live longer," she says. "We spend more years in employment and really have time for a couple of careers. So if a few years are taken out, all is not lost." The woman, by the way, is Supreme Court Justice Sandra Day O'Connor.

From my experience, this is absolutely right. My only recommendation is that if you intend to stop working while your kids are young, consider finding a way to keep your career on a low simmer so that you stay up to date on skills and keep your résumé current. If you haven't stepped all the way out for too long, it's much easier to get back in. You can do this in an infinite variety of ways, from working part-time in traditional jobs to volunteering. Not only does it keep your skills sharpened, but also it provides you with the confidence that you can gear up again when you're ready.

Looking back, I see many things I wish I had known about crafting a career that were counter to the traditional advice I was given. Most important? The goal is to find a role in the world that doesn't feel like work. This only happens when you identify the overlap between your skills, your passions, and the market. Not only is this the most fulfilling position, but by tapping into your passions in a constructive way, your work enriches your life. Finding the right opportunities requires experimenting along the way, trying lots of different alternatives, testing the messages you get both explicitly and implicitly from the world, and pushing back on those that just don't feel right.

As you move through your career, you will be well served by frequently reassessing where you are and where you want to go in the long run. Doing so allows you to make course corrections quickly, especially when things don't turn out as planned or exceptional new opportunities arise. Don't worry that the path ahead appears out of focus—squinting isn't going to make it any clearer. This is true for everyone. Don't be in a rush to get to your final destination—the side trips and unexpected detours quite often lead to the most interesting people, places, and opportunities. And, finally, be wary of all career advice, including mine, as you figure out what's right for you.

Chapter 8

Turn Lemonade into Helicopters

I called my son, Josh, during his first semester at college to wish him luck on his final exams. His response was "There's no such thing as luck. It's all hard work." He's a driven kid who throws himself at the things about which he is passionate, especially athletic competitions that require a tremendous amount of training and preparation. At first I thought his response was extreme. But on further reflection, I believe he had it right. Even when we think we're lucky, we've usually worked remarkably hard to put ourselves in that position.

I've watched Josh with admiration as he has strived to meet goals others might think impossible. At nineteen, he decided to try his hand at competitive powerlifting. This wasn't a natural choice for a former cyclist and track sprinter, but he was determined to break the national record for dead lifts. Josh identified the best trainers in Northern California and drove two hours each way, several times a week, to learn from them. He read everything he could about the sport, carefully crafted a diet to build more muscle, and spent hours training at the gym.

After several years of weight training, followed by months of focused effort, he entered a competition to see how he stacked up against others. We arose at 5:00 a.m. and drove three hours to Fresno for a formal meet. The gym was filled with weight lifters who'd been competing for years. I was worried he would be disappointed with his performance. But Josh, weighing in at 190 pounds, blew away both the state and national records of the federation by lifting 589.7 pounds (267.5 kilograms), 8 percent more than the previous record holder. Was he lucky? Of course he was lucky. All the cards aligned for him that day. But he would never have succeeded unless he had put tremendous effort behind his goals.

Josh's comment on luck echoed the message I frequently heard from my father when I was a child: the harder you work, the luckier you get. His mantra was a stark reminder that you need to put yourself in a position to be lucky. Even if there's a low probability of success and a tremendous amount of competition, you can maximize your chances by being well prepared physically, intellectually, and emotionally.

We often hear inspiring stories about people who start with nothing and by virtue of incredibly hard work are able to draw luck their way. I heard the following story from Quincy Jones III, aka QD3, which illustrates how this works.

As the son of the music legend Quincy Jones, you might think that QD3 had an easy life. He didn't. His parents divorced when he was young, and his mother brought him to Sweden, her native country, where they lived in near poverty. His mother had an alternative lifestyle and struggled with drug addiction. She didn't particularly care if QD3 went to school, and she often didn't come home from partying until four in the morning. He was essentially raising himself.

Spending lots of time on the streets, QD3 was exposed to break dancing, which was often performed on street corners. From the time he was exposed to it, he was hooked. He practiced hours each day, perfecting his moves, and soon started performing on the streets in Stockholm, putting out a hat to collect donations from passersby. One day a scout from Levi's saw him dancing on the street and asked if he would be interested in going on a performance tour. QD3 jumped at the chance!

Once he had his foot in the door, QD3 continued to work as hard as he could. Besides dancing, he started developing music beats for rap artists. A big break came when he was asked to write the soundtrack for a movie about the rap scene in Stockholm. One of his songs, "Next Time," written when he was sixteen, became his first gold record and sold more than 50,000 copies. QD3 went on to produce a triple-platinum documentary about Tupac Shakur, which sold more than 300,000 copies.

QD3 was driven to pull himself out of poverty, to be self-sufficient and, ultimately, the best in the world. He says that he "taps the fire in his heart" to motivate himself, and once the flame spreads, he charges ahead with incredible commitment and effort. He threw everything he had—physically, intellectually, and emotionally—at the problems confronting him, demonstrating that hard work and dedication are key to tempting luck your way.

I've learned that hard work is just one lever at your disposal when it comes to making your own luck. There are many other tools in your toolbox that can serve as luck magnets. And I'm confident that QD3 used these as well.

Luck is defined as "success or failure apparently brought by chance rather than through one's own actions."[1] *Apparently* — that is the operative word. In fact, each of us has a long list of levers at our disposal for unleashing good luck. However, luck *appears* to be brought on by chance because other people rarely see all those levers in action.

After years of observing what makes people successful, it is clear to me that good luck results from a definable list of tiny choices, micro behaviors, that allow people to squeeze just a little more juice out of every day, ultimately amplifying their long-term chances of success. Unfortunately, we usually look at others who have achieved remarkable things and point to a few very visible moments that unlocked opportunities for them.

Consider this example from Michael Lewis, the author of many very successful books, including *Liar's Poker* and *Moneyball*. During his commencement address at Princeton, he traced much of his success to luck.

> One night I was invited to a dinner, where I sat next to the wife of a big shot of a big Wall Street investment bank, Salomon Brothers. She more or less forced her husband to give me a job. I knew next to nothing about Salomon Brothers. But Salomon Brothers happened to be where Wall Street was being reinvented — into the Wall Street we've come to know and love today. When I got there I was assigned, almost arbitrarily, to the very best job in the place to observe the growing madness: they turned me into the house derivatives expert.

He used this experience to inspire and inform his 1989 best-seller *Liar's Poker*. He went on in his talk to attribute that success to luck:

> All of a sudden people were telling me I was a born writer. This was absurd. Even I could see that there was another, more true narrative, with luck as its theme. What were the odds of being seated at that dinner next to that Salomon Brothers lady? Of landing inside the best Wall Street firm to write the story of the age? Of landing in the seat with the best view of the business?[2]

Not so fast. Don't be fooled by this simple version of the story. There were countless things that Michael Lewis needed to do before, during, and after the conversation with the woman at the dinner party that set him up for success. Focusing just on that chance meeting distracts us from what *really* happened. Yes, he was fortunate to sit next to someone who was influential in helping him get a job at Salomon Brothers. But hundreds of people sat next to that woman over the years, and she didn't convince her husband to hire them. And thousands of people worked at Salomon Brothers, and none of them wrote a bestseller about their experience.

What set up Michael Lewis to see and seize this opportunity? A well-known quote from the famous scientist Louis Pasteur states, "Chance favors the prepared mind." This is absolutely true. But what exactly is a *prepared* mind? What makes us receptive to chance events and able to capitalize on them?

There is "physics" to luck, since all of life is a matter of cause and effect. This can be compared to the relationship between our genetics and our environment in determining who we become. As we now know, both are instrumental in shaping us, and they are deeply intertwined—our genetics influences how we engage with our environment, and our environment influences which traits are expressed. The same is true with luck and our behavior. Luck captures the things that happen *to us*, and our behavior encapsulates the things over which *we have control*. We can debate which comes first, but in the end, they are inexorably connected.

We are locked in a continuous dance with the world in which we trade off who is leading and who is following. Once the dance begins, we have immense control over our luck because it is a direct result of our behavior. We certainly can't control everything that happens to us, but we can control our responses. Luck results when we know how and when to lead in our dance with life. For example, in Michael Lewis's story, he randomly sat next to the woman at dinner and took advantage of that opportunity to impress her enough that she introduced him to her husband. He was a *follower* when he sat down and became a *leader* when he engaged the woman in conversation, resulting in future opportunities to lead and to follow. And we can be sure that during the process of writing his books, and his involvement in the movies based on them, that there were hundreds of times when he shifted from follower to leader as surprising events occurred along the way.

The dance we do in life includes several partners—the world, other people, and ourselves. We are, therefore, doing several dances at once. This is complicated because the dances also influence one another. By understanding the underlying physics of these relationships, we are much better *prepared* to unleash luck.

Don't be distracted by the way the word "luck" is used in everyday jargon. Often it is deployed as an excuse. For example, people frequently attribute their successes to luck, saying they're "lucky" to modestly mask the skills they've mobilized. And we give others and ourselves a break by blaming poor performance on bad luck. A careful observer will look behind the curtain to see what actually happened and whether it was fortune, chance, or luck.

It is important to define these terms, which are often used interchangeably. They are actually quite different, especially as they relate to "agency"—or the amount of personal control we have over each one.

> **FORTUNE** is something that happens *to you*. It is good fortune to be born into a kind family and bad fortune to be struck by lightning.
>
> **CHANCE** requires an action on your part. You need to *take a chance*, such as rolling dice, buying a lottery ticket, or asking someone out on a date, to benefit from a chance event.
>
> **LUCK** is made by finding and creating opportunities. It is a *direct consequence* of your behavior. For example, you're *lucky* that you were offered a great job. There was a lot of agency, even though there was uncertainty. You had to do the work to build the skills to be prepared and to actively apply for that role.

The fact that we conflate the terms "fortune," "chance," and "luck" speaks to the fact that most people aren't fully aware of how much control they have over their fate. They attribute events to randomness—*bad or good luck*—when really they have much more influence than they acknowledge. If you look closely, you will see lots of tiny choices that add up over time. Each one sets the stage for the things that occur in the future. Consider the following conversation between colleagues, with four different trajectories:

Conversation 1

Sarah: Hello, how are you?
Joe: Great, how are you?
Sarah: I'm way too busy, and really stressed.
Joe: You work too hard.

Conversation 2

Sarah: Hello, how are you?
Joe: Great, how are you?
Sarah: I'm way too busy, and really stressed.
Joe: So sorry to hear that.

Conversation 3

Sarah: Hello, how are you?
Joe: Great, how are you?
Sarah: I'm way too busy, and really stressed.
Joe: Is there anything I can do to be helpful?

Conversation 4

Sarah: Hello, how are you?
Joe: Great, how are you?
Sarah: I'm way too busy, and really stressed.
Joe: Would it be helpful if I take care of X for you?

These may seem like similar conversations, but they aren't. Sarah will have a completely different attitude and relationship with Joe after each of these scenarios. As you move from the first to the last interaction, Joe has more empathy and is ultimately offering to solve Sarah's problem in a very specific way. If Sarah is really stressed, having Joe offer to help significantly shifts their relationship, and she is much more likely to help Joe in the future if he helps her now.

Of course, if Joe responds as portrayed in scenarios 1 or 2, he isn't going to get fired. But he has missed an opportunity to build trust with Sarah. After months and years, he probably won't even see all the opportunities he missed. In scenarios 3 and 4, Joe builds a meaningful relationship with Sarah. And, not surprisingly, as opportunities arise, she is more likely to offer them to Joe. Others might not see the small things Joe has done and will look at his progression as just good fortune. In reality, by helping others, others are more likely to help us.

The opportunity to build a trusting relationship with others happens hundreds of times each day. Heidi Roizen, a successful entrepreneur and venture capitalist, shared a particularly memorable example in one of our classes. She had just dropped off her child at college and was much more affected by the experience than she thought she would be. Teary-eyed, she arrived at a meeting she had set up immediately afterward with a fellow who wanted to pitch her his new company. Heidi mentioned that she was very emotional after dropping her child at college. Instead of responding in a caring and empathetic way, he opened his laptop and started in on his pitch. She was amazed—he had missed the opportunity to be compassionate. She walked away knowing that she would never do business with this fellow. Had he taken a few minutes to ask her about the experience and to offer some kind words, it would have dramatically shifted the way she viewed him and his venture.

•   •   •

Essentially, by understanding the physics of luck we are much more prepared to identify and capture opportunities that lead us to our desired goals, allowing us to thrive, not just survive. The following 2 × 2 matrix illustrates the different ways people engage with the world, allowing them to see and seize opportunities—or not.

Those in the *upper left quadrant* see possibilities but don't act on them, leaving it to others. They are observant enough to identify opportunities but don't execute on those ideas. They watch others succeed and are likely to say "I could have done that" or "I thought of that idea, too." They end up bitter because they saw the opportunity but didn't act on it.

Those in the *bottom right quadrant* seize opportunities without paying careful attention to the environment and act blindly without fully comprehending the situation. For example, they start a business without understanding their customers' real needs. As a result, they're surprised and disappointed when their ideas don't pan out or have less-than-optimal results.

Those in the *lower left quadrant*—who don't see or seize possibilities—don't pay attention or act on opportunities, sitting on the sidelines of life. They watch others get ahead and are baffled that opportunities seem to pass them by. They are clueless.

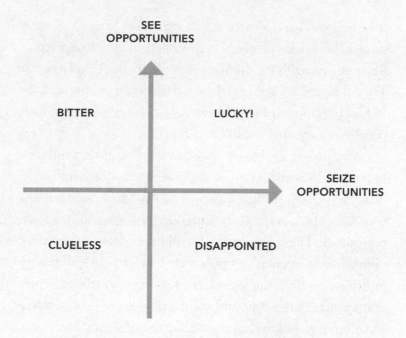

Those in the *upper right quadrant,* who pay careful attention to identify opportunities *and* find ways to act on them, are "lucky." They move through the world seeing and seizing opportunities.

There are ways to move into the upper right quadrant. Richard Wiseman, of the University of Hertfordshire in England, has studied luck and found that "lucky people" share traits that tend to make them luckier than others. First, he recognized that lucky people take advantage of chance occurrences that come their way. Instead of going through life on cruise control, they pay attention to what's happening around them and, therefore, are able to extract greater value from each situation. They're more likely to pay attention to an announcement for a special event in their community, to notice a new person in their neighborhood, or to see that a friend is in need of some extra help. Lucky people are also open to novel opportunities and willing to try things outside their usual experiences. They're more inclined to pick up a book on an unfamiliar subject, to travel to less familiar destinations, and to interact with people who are different from them.

Lucky people tend to be optimistic and expect good things to happen to them. They make more eye contact and smile more frequently, leading to more positive and extended encounters. These actions, in turn, open the door to more opportunities. These become self-fulfilling prophecies, because even when things don't go as expected, lucky people find ways to extract positive outcomes from the worst situations. Their attitude affects those around them and helps to turn negative situations into positive experiences. In short, being observant, open-minded, friendly, and optimistic invites luck your way.

This simple story shows how this works. Several years ago I was at a small, local grocery store frequented mostly by those who live nearby. A man and his young daughter approached me in the frozen-food aisle and politely asked how to prepare frozen, canned lemonade. The man had an accent I couldn't identify, and I was pretty sure he must be new to the area. I told him how to prepare the lemonade and asked where he was from. He said Santiago, Chile. I asked his name and what brought him to our town. I had no ulterior motive. I was just curious. He told me his name was Eduardo and that he and his family were in the area for a year so he could learn about entrepreneurship in Silicon Valley. He was in line to run his family's business and was in search of tools to make it more innovative. I told him about our entrepreneurship program at Stanford's

School of Engineering and said I'd be happy to do what I could to be of help. Over the next few months I introduced Eduardo to various people in the entrepreneurship community, and he expressed his thanks for my assistance.

Fast-forward two years. I was heading to a conference in Santiago, Chile, and sent Eduardo a message asking if he wanted to get together for coffee. At the last minute, he wasn't able to make it but invited me to go to a specific location in downtown Santiago with a few of my colleagues. We showed up at the office building and were led to the roof, where we were picked up by Eduardo's family's private helicopter for a simply spectacular ride above the city, up to the surrounding mountains, and over his family's ski resort. It was incredible! And to think that it resulted from helping him figure out how to make lemonade. Of course, I didn't help Eduardo because I wanted a helicopter ride. But by putting myself out there, being open to helping someone, and following up years later, I became quite "lucky." Earlier I discussed the art of turning lemons (problems) into lemonade (opportunities). But luck goes beyond this—it's about turning lemonade (good things) into helicopters (amazing things!).

On the other hand, there are people who are truly unlucky. They aren't observant, are close-minded, unfriendly, and pessimistic. There is a video, called "The Secret of Luck,"[3] set in the small West Yorkshire town of Todmorden, that demonstrates this. As part of the film, the producers followed a man, named Wayne, who claimed that he was terribly unlucky. They then observed how Wayne engaged with the world around him.

It became clear that Wayne really was unlucky. Even when the producers put all sorts of lucky opportunities in his path, he missed them all. For example, Wayne was a butcher, and they approached him on the street pretending to be doing a market survey. The survey was about cuts of meat, and there was a cash prize. He didn't participate and missed out. They put a winning scratcher lottery ticket in his mailbox. If he had scratched it, he would have won a television. He didn't. Instead, he looked at it and threw it away. He missed out again. And they literally put a fifty-pound note on the sidewalk, and he walked right over it. Finally, out of desperation to get his attention, they put an enormous sign on the side of a truck that said, WAYNE, CALL THIS NUMBER . . . They had to follow him around town all day before he *finally* saw it and made the call. He was prompted to leave a voice mail message. Later, the producers showed up and told him all the things they had done to tempt luck his way. He immediately realized that his lack of good luck was very much self-imposed.

Essentially, the world is full of doors through which we can find a staggering array of opportunities—we just have to be willing to open them. Carlos Vignolo, from the University of Chile, likes to say that if you go somewhere and don't meet someone new, you have missed out on making a friend as well as the possibility of making a million dollars. He tells his students that every time they walk onto a city bus, a million dollars is waiting there for them—they just have to find it. In this case "a million dollars" is a metaphor for learning something new, making a friend, or, indeed, making money. In fact, this book is the direct result of my talking with someone sitting next to me on an airplane, as I describe in my letter at the end of this book. If I hadn't started that conversation, it's unlikely this book would exist.

• • •

We are faced with large and small opportunities to make our own luck every moment of every day. In fact, luck is not like a lightning strike but more like the wind. With the right attitude and tools, you build a sail that captures luck as it blows by. That wind is constantly blowing—sometimes lightly, sometimes in gusts, and sometimes in directions you didn't anticipate. When your sail is up, you are always ready. Even when the wind is negligible, it can be used to guide you slowly toward your objectives. And when the wind picks up, you are ready![4]

There are dozens of possibilities in every situation, and it is up to you to see and seize some of them. The trick here is that opportunities don't have red flashing neon signs on them. Echoing this point, Tom Kelley, author of *The Art of Innovation*, says that every day you should act like a foreign traveler by being acutely aware of your environment. In everyday life we tend to put on blinders and cruise down well-worn paths, rarely stopping to look around. But as a traveler in a foreign country, you see the world with fresh eyes and dramatically increase the density of your experiences. By tuning in, you find fascinating things around every turn.

James Barlow, the former head of the Scottish Institute for Enterprise, did a provocative exercise with his students to demonstrate this point. He gave jigsaw puzzles to several teams and set a timer to see which group would finish first. Each piece had secretly been numbered on the back, from 1 to 500, so it would be relatively easy to put them together if one paid attention to the numbers. But even though the numbers were right in front of them, it took most teams a very long time to see them, and some never saw them at all. They could have easily bolstered their luck just by paying closer attention.

I do a simple exercise in my class that illustrates this clearly. I send students to a familiar location, such as the local shopping center, and ask them to complete a "lab" in which they go to several stores and pay attention to all the things that are normally "invisible." They take the time to notice the sounds, smells, textures, and colors, as well as the organization of the merchandise and the way the staff interacts with the customers. They observe things they'd never seen when they had previously zipped in and out of the same environment. They come back with their eyes wide open, realizing that we all tend to walk through life with blinders on.

Lucky people don't just pay attention to the world around them and meet interesting individuals; they also find unusual ways to use and recombine their knowledge and experiences. Most people have remarkable resources at their fingertips but never figure out how to leverage them. However, lucky people appreciate the value of their knowledge and their network, and tap into these gold mines as needed. Here's a powerful example from the 2005 commencement address that Steve Jobs delivered at Stanford. In short, he dropped out of college after six months because he wasn't sure why he was there, and the tuition was much more than his parents could afford. Here's how Steve tells it:

> Reed College at that time offered perhaps the best calligraphy instruction in the country. Throughout the campus every poster, every label on every drawer, was beautifully hand calligraphed. Because I had dropped

out and didn't have to take the normal classes, I decided to take a calligraphy class to learn how to do this. I learned about serif and sans serif typefaces, about varying the amount of space between different letter combinations, about what makes great typography great. It was beautiful, historical, artistically subtle in a way that science can't capture, and I found it fascinating.

None of this had even a hope of any practical application in my life. But ten years later, when we were designing the first Macintosh computer, it all came back to me. And we designed it all into the Mac. It was the first computer with beautiful typography. . . . Of course it was impossible to connect the dots looking forward when I was in college. But it was very, very clear looking backwards ten years later.[5]

This story emphasizes that you never know when your experiences will prove to be valuable. Steve Jobs was open-minded and curious about the world, collected diverse experiences independent of their short-term benefits, and was able to tap into his knowledge in unexpected ways. This is a sharp reminder that the more experiences you have and the broader your base of knowledge, the more resources you have from which to draw.

In my course on creativity I focus a great deal on the value of recombining ideas in unusual ways. The more you practice this skill, the more natural it becomes. For example, using similes or metaphors to describe concepts that on the surface seem completely unrelated offers tools for revealing fresh solutions to familiar problems. We do a simple exercise to illustrate

this point. Teams are asked to come up with as many answers
as possible to the following statement:

Ideas are like _____ *because* _____,
therefore _____.

Below is a list of some of the hundreds of creative answers
I've seen. In each case the simile unlocks a new way of looking
at ideas:

- Ideas are like babies because everyone thinks theirs
  is cute, therefore be objective when judging your
  own ideas.
- Ideas are like shoes because you need to break them
  in, therefore take time to evaluate new ideas.
- Ideas are like mirrors because they reflect the local
  environment, therefore consider changing contexts
  to get more diverse collections of ideas.
- Ideas are like hiccups because when they start they
  don't stop, therefore take advantage of idea streaks.
- Ideas are like bubbles because they easily burst,
  therefore be gentle with them.
- Ideas are like cars because they take you places,
  therefore go along for the ride.
- Ideas are like chocolates because everyone loves
  them, therefore make sure to serve them up
  frequently.
- Ideas are like the measles because they are
  contagious, therefore hang out with other people
  with ideas if you want to get them yourself.
- Ideas are like waffles because they are best when
  fresh, therefore keep new ideas coming all the time.

- Ideas are like spiderwebs because they are stronger than they appear, therefore don't underestimate them.

This exercise encourages you to stretch your imagination by tapping into the world around you for inspiration. Some people make these connections naturally and find unusual ways to extract value from them. Like Steve Jobs, those people are always scouting for how to bring ideas together in interesting ways and then make the effort to bring their ideas to life.

A couple of stories illustrate how this works in real life. Perry Klebahn broke his ankle in 1991. The injury was especially disappointing to this avid skier, who didn't want to miss a season on the slopes. However, he found a way to turn his bad fortune into good luck. While recovering from the injury, he discovered an old pair of wooden snowshoes and took them out for a spin, hoping this would provide an alternative to skiing. They didn't work well at all, which was another disappointment. But instead of throwing them back into his closet and waiting for his ankle to heal, Perry decided to design a new snowshoe. He was a product design student at the time and figured he could use these new skills to solve his own problem. Over the course of ten weeks, he designed and built eight different versions of snowshoes. On weekdays he built prototypes in the school machine shop, and over weekends he went to the mountains to try them out. By the end of the tenth week, he was ready to file patents on his invention.

Once the design was perfected, Perry hand-built some snowshoes and set out to sell them to sporting goods stores. The buyers took one look at them and asked, "What are these?"

They were unlike anything they had seen before, and there was *no* market for snowshoes. But Perry persevered, knowing there must be lots of people who couldn't ski for one reason or another but still wanted a way to spend time in the mountains during the winter. In the end, he decided to build the market himself.

Perry personally took sporting goods salespeople to the snow-covered mountains each weekend to let them try out his invention. He told them there was no obligation to promote snowshoes to their customers; he just wanted them to get a taste of this new sport. The salespeople loved the experience and passed the news on to the buyers at their stores. As a result, sporting goods stores started stocking Perry's new product. But the challenge didn't stop there.

After customers purchased Perry's new snowshoes, they had no clue where to use them. So Perry had to convince ski resorts around the United States to promote snowshoeing. He encouraged them to create special snowshoe trails, to make maps for their customers, to provide trail passes, and to monitor the trails to keep them safe. Once this was done, the pieces were in place for the market for his snowshoes to balloon, and it grew from $0 to $50 million. Perry's company, Atlas Snowshoe, was subsequently sold to K2, and snowshoes and well-marked trails for snowshoeing are now widely available.

Perry turned a series of bad breaks—literal and figurative— into a winning streak by seeing opportunities and connecting the dots between his broken ankle, his desire to spend time in the snow, his new product design skills, and his astute observation that others would benefit from a better snowshoe. He ultimately made out well, but only after huge investments of time, energy, and perseverance. Many people would have given up along the way, balking or even stopping at each new obstacle. But Perry saw opportunities in every challenge, and as each hurdle was overcome and all the pieces were put in place, his chances of seeing a positive end result increased. This only happened because Perry used every skill described by Richard Wiseman. He was observant, outgoing, adventurous, and optimistic, as well as hardworking. Each of these traits was important in contributing to his ultimate goal.

While Perry worked incredibly hard to overcome obstacles to create his own luck, there are many examples of individuals making luck by fearlessly asking for what they want. A compelling example is found in Dana Calderwood's story. Dana loved the theater and spent countless hours involved in school plays, starting when he was in high school. We were classmates at Summit High School in New Jersey, where we were both serious "drama freaks." Acting was a hobby for me, but Dana had dreams of being a director and started cooking up his own luck in order to optimize the chances of making that happen long before he left high school.

Dana was fearless. He had the gumption to ask the head of the drama department if he could direct the next major school play. No student had ever asked for that role before, but the teacher agreed. Dana didn't wait to be anointed by someone in authority; he simply asked for what he wanted. That moment launched Dana's directing career. He went on to direct plays at the local Metropolitan Musical Theater, where a visiting alumni director, who had since gone on to a successful career in Hollywood, gave him some sage advice. He told Dana that the skills he was using at the theater company were the same skills needed in the big leagues. This advice gave Dana the confidence to set his sights even higher.

Dana went on to study at New York University's film school, and while there, he squeezed the juice out of every opportunity. Dana always stayed after classes to meet guest speakers, and he asked them for follow-up meetings and names of other people he should contact. He also learned to make the most of every film assignment. At first, like his classmates, he used his friends as actors in his films (this is how I got my film debut in Dana's version of the famous shower scene in *Psycho*). However, Dana soon realized there was an opportunity to invite famous actors to star in his pieces. One TV production class assignment involved creating a short program for television. Most of Dana's classmates conducted simple interviews with one another to satisfy the requirement, but Dana asked the Academy Award–winning actress Estelle Parsons, who was in the midst of performing in a Tony-nominated play, to participate—and she agreed. Again, he made himself lucky by paying attention to non-obvious but exciting alternatives. He put himself out there by asking for what he wanted.

As time went on, Dana took on bigger and bigger challenges, and eventually he was asked to be the director of *Late Night with Conan O'Brien*, which he did for years before moving on to direct many other shows, including *Rachael Ray* and *Iron Chef America*. Had Dana seen his adult self when he was twenty, he would have been in awe of his good luck. Dana's fortune comes from putting everything he knows into everything he does. He is fearless about asking for opportunities to do things he has never done before, and with each successful leap, he gains additional insights and knowledge that help him take on the next bigger challenge.

Dana long ago internalized the idea that directing on a small stage is similar to directing on a big stage, and this gave him the confidence to jump to ever-larger stepping-stones as he literally made opportunities present themselves. Many people don't feel comfortable making such leaps, preferring instead to stay in smaller venues. And one could argue that there are many advantages to working with intimate teams on small projects. Others dream of a bigger stage but are daunted by the perceived distance between where they are and where they want to go. Dana's story shows that by seeing and seizing all the opportunities around us, we can slowly but surely pull ourselves from stage to stage, each time drawing ourselves closer to our final objective.

We can all manufacture our own luck by understanding that luck is like the wind—always blowing. It is up to you to catch the winds of luck by being open to opportunities that come your way, taking full advantage of chance occurrences, paying careful attention to the world around you, interacting with as many people as you can, and making those interactions as positive as possible. Making one's own luck is ultimately about turning bad situations around and making good situations much better. We dramatically increase the chances that we will be lucky by exposing ourselves to as many diverse experiences as possible, boldly recombining these experiences in unusual ways, and fearlessly striving to get to the stage on which we want to play out our lives.

Chapter 9

Are You Smart or Right?

Who would have thought that the package of note cards my mother gave me for my tenth birthday would have been one of the most valuable gifts I have ever received. They were light blue and said TINA in block letters on the top. My mother taught me at that age how to write a thank-you note and how important they are. She couldn't have been more correct. In fact, as I grew up and ultimately entered the work world, I often tried to channel my mother, who always seemed to know what to do in social settings. But the importance of writing thank-you notes remains one of her most valuable lessons.

Since then I've learned that there is a big difference between gratitude and appreciation: gratitude is the quality of *being* thankful, and appreciation is the act of *showing* gratitude. Research has proven that gratitude leads to improved mental and physical health, better sleep, and increased productivity. But gratitude is not enough—you need to acknowledge those who have done something for you in order to get the full benefit.

Keep in mind that everything someone does for you has an opportunity cost. That means if someone takes time out of his or her day to attend to you, there's something they haven't done for themselves or for someone else. It's easy to fool yourself into thinking your request is small. But when someone is busy there are no small requests. They have to stop what they're doing, focus on your request, and take the time to respond. With that in mind, there is never a time when you shouldn't thank someone for doing something for you. In fact, assume a thank-you note is in order, and look at situations when you don't send one as the exception. Because so few people actually do this (unfortunately), you will certainly stand out from the crowd.

I've been experimenting with different ways of expressing appreciation and developed a new habit as a result. At the end of every day, I review my calendar and send a short thank-you email to everyone who has done something helpful, such as meeting with me to discuss a project or taking me to lunch. It takes only a few minutes, but it forces me to consider all the things that others have done for me. This single act increases my gratitude and appreciation, and certainly makes a big difference in my relationships with others.

There are many other little things that make a big difference. Some are intuitive, and others are surprising. Some are taught in schools, but most are not. Over the years, I've stumbled many times, sometimes irreversibly, by not understanding these "little things."

First and foremost, remember that there are only fifty people in the world. Of course, this isn't true literally. But it often feels that way because you're likely to bump into people you know, or people who know the people you know, all over the world. The person sitting next to you might become your boss, your employee, your customer, or your sister-in-law. Over the course of your life, the same people will quite likely play many different roles. I've had many occasions in which individuals who were once my superiors later came to me for help, and I've found myself going to people who were once my subordinates for guidance. The roles we play continue to change in surprising ways over time, and you will be amazed by the people who keep showing up in your life.

Because we live in such a small world, it really is important to build bridges—and never to burn them no matter how tempted you might be. You aren't going to like everyone and everyone isn't going to like you, but there's no need to make enemies. For example, when you look for your next job, it's quite likely that the person interviewing you will know someone you know. In this way your reputation precedes you everywhere you go. This is beneficial when you have a great reputation but harmful when your reputation is damaged.

I've seen the following scenario play out innumerable times. Imagine you're interviewing for a job that has dozens of candidates. The interview goes well, and you appear to be a great match for the position. During the meeting, the interviewer looks at your résumé and realizes that you used to work with an old friend of hers. After the interview, she makes a quick call to her friend to ask about you. A casual comment from her friend about your past performance can seal the deal or cut you off at the knees. In many cases you will believe the job was in the bag, right before you receive a rejection letter. You'll never know what hit you.

Your reputation is your most valuable asset, so guard it well. But don't be terribly demoralized if you make some mistakes along the way. With time, it is possible to repair a stained reputation. Over the years, I've come up with a metaphor that has helped me put this in perspective: Every experience you have with someone else is a drop of water falling into a pool. As your experiences with that person grow, the drops accumulate and the pool deepens. Positive interactions are clear drops of water, and negative interactions are red drops of water. But they aren't equal. That is, a number of clear drops can dilute one red drop, and that number differs for different people. Those who are very forgiving only need a few positive experiences—clear drops—to dilute a bad experience, while those who are less forgiving need a lot more to wash away the red. Also, the pool drains at different rates for different people. As a result, some people only pay attention to the experiences that have happened most recently, while others hold on to good and bad experiences for a very long time.

This metaphor implies that if you have a large reserve of positive experiences with someone, then one red drop is hardly noticed. It's like putting a drop of red ink into the ocean. But if you don't know a person well, one or two bad experiences stain the pool bright red. You can wash away negative interactions by flooding the pool with positive interactions until the red drops fade, but the deeper the red, the more work you have to do to cleanse the pool. I've found that sometimes the pool color never clears. When that happens, it's time to stop interacting with that particular person.

This serves as a reminder of the importance of every experience we have with others, whether they are friends, family members, coworkers, or service providers. In fact, some organizations actually capture information about how you treat them, and that influences how they treat you. For example, at some well-known business schools every interaction a candidate has with the school or its personnel is noted. If a candidate is rude to the receptionist, this is recorded in his or her file and comes into play when admissions decisions are made. This also happens at companies such as JetBlue. According to Bob Sutton in his book *The No Asshole Rule*, if you're consistently rude to JetBlue's staff, you will get blacklisted and find it strangely impossible to get a seat on their planes.[1]

Obviously, you can't make everyone happy all the time, and some of your actions are going to ruffle feathers. One way to figure out how to handle these situations is to imagine how you will describe what happened later, when the dust has cleared. I'm reminded of a case a few years ago when a student came to me for advice. He was leading the campus-wide business plan competition, and one team hadn't shown up for the final round of judging. Like all the teams that reach that stage of the competition, the team had been working on the project for seven months and had managed to make it over a lot of hurdles to get to the finish line. The team hadn't received the message about the presentation time, in part because it was posted late and in part because they weren't paying attention.

The student who came to ask my opinion was torn about what to do. He felt there were two clear choices: he could hold fast to the rules and disqualify the team or he could be flexible and find another time for them to present their work. His gut reaction was to stick to the rules. Everyone else had managed to show up, and it was going to be a burden to reschedule. The only guidance I gave him was this: whatever he did, I hoped he would be pleased with his decision at a later date. I urged him to consider how he would describe this challenge if during a job interview he were asked how he handled an ambiguous situation, or what he would tell his child about this experience years in the future. The delinquent team was subsequently allowed to present. Remember, thinking about how you want to tell the story in the future is a great way to assess your response to dilemmas in general. Craft the story now so you'll be proud to tell it later.

•   •   •

Everyone makes mistakes, and floundering is part of life, especially when you're doing things for the first time. I've spent countless hours kicking myself for stupid things I've done. However, I've also figured out that learning how to recover from those mistakes is key. For instance, knowing how to apologize is incredibly important. A simple acknowledgment that you messed up goes a long way. There's no need for long speeches and explanations; just say, "I didn't handle that very well. I apologize, and I won't do that again." The sooner you do this after recognizing your mistake, the better. If you wait a long time to apologize, the damage continues to grow.

I've had many chances to practice recovering from errors. This story is particularly memorable: Soon after I got out of school, I read an article in the local newspaper about plans to build the San Jose Tech Museum of Innovation. It sounded like it would be an amazing place to work. Jim Adams, a Stanford professor known for his pioneering work on creativity, would be the museum's director. I called the museum office daily in an attempt to reach him but each time was told Jim wasn't there. Although I didn't leave messages, the receptionist learned to recognize my voice and informed Jim every time I called. By the time I reached him, Jim had a stack of messages from me that was nearly an inch tall.

Jim finally agreed to meet with me. I managed to pass the test with him during the interview, but there really was no formal job to offer me, and he ultimately suggested I talk with the woman who had recently been hired to lead the exhibit design effort. It's not unlikely that her first assignment was to get rid of me. She invited me to lunch for an interview, but before we'd even ordered she said, "I just want to tell you that you're not a good match for this organization. You're just too pushy." I felt tears welling up and had to think fast to pull out of the tailspin. I apologized, told her I appreciated the feedback, and said that most people would call me high energy and enthusiastic. Clearly, my enthusiasm had been misinterpreted. The tension melted, we had a fascinating conversation, and I walked away with a job offer.

This story demonstrates that it is important to take responsibility for your actions and be willing to learn from your experiences. Once that happens, you can quickly move on. And echoing an earlier point, the course I now teach on creativity at Stanford was pioneered by Jim Adams many years ago. It really is a very small world!

Jeannie Kahwajy, an expert on interpersonal interactions, performed research that shows that those who demonstrate that they are willing to learn can turn negative situations around very effectively. Jeannie ran experiments involving mock interviews by recruiters of job candidates. The recruiter was primed beforehand to have a negative bias toward the candidate. Of the three groups of candidates, one was instructed to *prove* they should get the job, one was told to *learn* from the interaction, and the final group, the control, was given no specific instructions. She found that the recruiter's negative bias was reinforced for both the control group and the group that tried to prove they should get the job. However, the candidates who set out to learn from the interaction reversed the recruiter's negative bias. What an insight! A mindset of learning is powerful enough to change someone's negative bias toward you.

Another valuable skill is the art of helping others. When I was in college I spoke with my parents about once a week. At the end of every call my mother would say, "What can I do to be helpful to you?" The generosity of this gesture made a huge impression on me. In most cases there was nothing she could do to be helpful, but just knowing she was willing to help if needed was comforting. As I got older, I realized we all can do this for our friends, family, and colleagues. When you ask others if you can help, they are always pleased that you offered. A small number will actually take you up on your offer, and the things they ask for are usually modest. On rare occasions, someone will ask for something you can't or don't want to do. Even when you turn them down, they are grateful that you offered and graciously accept the fact that you aren't able to help. This concept is also discussed in the chapter on making your own luck, since the more you help others, the luckier you get.

I suggest that you try this sometime, if you don't do it routinely already. But you must be sincerely willing to help if your offer is accepted. As Guy Kawasaki says, "You should always try to be a 'mensch.'" He continues, "A mensch helps people who cannot help them. A mensch is not motivated by the fact of 'Wow! This person is the western regional manager for the

Wall Street Journal, and if I suck up to this *Wall Street Journal* person, maybe I will get some good press. This person can help me, therefore I will help them.' A mensch does not think like that. A mensch thinks, 'I will help people for the sheer pleasure of helping people.' You know, a waiter cannot really do much for you. I guess they could bring your food, but you know besides that, they cannot do very much. You want to see a good test for a mensch? Watch how they treat waiters, and waitresses, and flight attendants. . . . Ultimately, at the end of one's life, you are judged not by your market share, not whether you beat the US Department of Justice Antitrust Division, not because you had the most German cars, or Italian cars. You are judged by, 'Did you make the world a better place?' "[2]

I clearly remember when I didn't know how to do this. When I was a freshman in college there was a fellow in my class who had a physical disability that required him to use crutches to walk. One day he slipped walking down a ramp to class and fell to the ground. As he was struggling to get up, I didn't know what to do. I felt uncomfortable walking by without helping, but I was afraid that if I approached him I would embarrass him by drawing attention to his disability. I felt the same way when a classmate lost his mother to a long illness. I didn't know what to say, fearing I would say something wrong, and opted to say nothing. Years later, I was running on campus at Stanford. It had rained the day before, and I slipped and fell hard in some mud. Bruised, hurt, and muddy, I sat on the curb with tears streaming down my face. At least a dozen people walked by, and not one asked me if I needed anything. At that exact moment I knew what I should have said to the fellow who had fallen in front of class years earlier and to my classmate who had lost his mother. All I needed was someone to ask, "Are you all right? Is there anything I can do for you?" It now seems so simple. It's remarkable that it took me so many years to figure this out.

In fact, a dear friend of mine had to school me on this. When she called me to tell me that she had just been diagnosed with breast cancer, I was certainly upset. But I didn't know what to do and didn't do anything. A week or so later, she called me again and asked what happened. She wondered if I was too upset to reach out, or if something else was going on. I told her honestly that I didn't know what to do and asked for guidance. She told me that she'd appreciate it if I would call her every day to check in. No problem! I could do that. I ended up calling her daily for eight years, before she sadly passed away. The advice she gave me was a huge gift. Not only did she teach me how to be helpful to her during such a difficult time, but our friendship flourished with daily contact. Some days we talked for only a few minutes, but that daily contact dramatically changed the texture of our relationship, and for that I am eternally grateful.

There is another big pothole that people often fall into: they rationalize doing the "smart" thing as opposed to the "right" thing. These two concepts are often confused. Intelligent people often overanalyze a problem, coming up with a solution they think is in their best interest (the smart choice) but isn't the right thing to do. Randy Komisar told a personal story to illustrate the point. He had a contractor who had worked on his house. The contractor did a terrible job, and the project required a lot of follow-up work to correct the mistakes. Long after the project was completed, the contractor called Randy and told him that he hadn't paid the final bill. Knowing how disorganized the contractor was, Randy was fairly confident he would never be able to prove this one way or another. But looking back over his own records, Randy found that indeed he had not paid the bill. It would have been easy to question the contractor's bookkeeping and to justify not paying the bill. However, Randy knew that, despite his frustration with the contractor's work, he owed the contractor the money. He wrote a check, knowing that it was the right thing to do.

When I think about doing the right thing instead of the smart thing, I'm reminded of a legal case in which I served as a juror. It was a wrongful termination case, in which a woman accused her employer of firing her without cause just days before her stock options were going to vest. This case went on for ten very long weeks, and I had a lot of time to think about the "right" outcome. The law was on the employer's side, because the plaintiff was an "at will" employee who could be fired at any time, but it wasn't clear whether the employer had done the "right" thing with regard to the timing of her dismissal. The jury deliberated for days. In retrospect, the deliberation was so difficult because we were torn between the right and the smart decision. Ultimately, we ruled in favor of the plaintiff, but we gave her a much smaller award than she was requesting. I later learned that the judgment was appealed, and another trial ensued.

Both the contractor and the trial stories highlight the fact that there is a significant difference between doing the right thing and rationalizing a decision that's best for you. Your actions always affect how others see you, and as mentioned innumerable times now, you will likely bump into these same people again. If nothing else, you can be sure they will remember how you handled yourself.

•   •   •

One of the biggest things people do to get in their own way is to take on way too many commitments. This eventually leads to frustration all the way around. Life is a huge buffet of enticing platters of possibilities, but putting too much on your plate just leads to indigestion. Just like a real buffet, in life you *can* do it all, just not at the same time. In fact, no matter your age, prioritizing is hard work. But as Greg McKeown says, "If you don't prioritize your life, someone else will."[3] The problem is that many of us grow up with a mindset of scarcity and end up in a world of abundance. As a result, when opportunities become more abundant, we gorge ourselves at the buffet, taking on much more than we can chew.[4]

One approach is to pick three priorities at any one time, knowing that these will change as your life changes. This concept is not new. In fact, the US Marine Corps and other military services use the Rule of Three as a general principle. Through years of trial and error, they've found that most people can track only three things at once. As a result, the entire military system is designed to reflect this. A squad leader is in charge of three fire team leaders, a platoon leader is in charge of three squad leaders, and each company consists of three platoons. The military experimented with a Rule of Four, and effectiveness dropped precipitously.

There is another way to look at the things on your to-do list: What things do you *need to do*, and what things do you *want to do*?

- It's easy to say yes to the things you need *and* want to do, such as attending a close friend's wedding.
- It's easy to say no to the things you neither want *nor* need to do, such as going to a meeting that isn't directly related to your work.
- You have to say yes to the things you need to do but don't want to do, such as filling out an expense report or taking out the garbage.
- The most challenging decisions involve the things that you want to do but don't need to do. In some cases the opportunity is so tempting that you may ultimately say yes, even though you are going to have to manufacture time to make it work.

It is important to train yourself to say no when you know deep down that you don't have the time, no matter how attractive the opportunity. In these cases I write a note with the following words: *Thank you so much for the wonderful opportunity. I wish I had time to participate. Please don't interpret my lack of time for a lack of interest.* This short message captures how much I appreciate the invitation and opens the door to potential future opportunities. It helps me to stay focused on the things that are the most important to me, as opposed to getting distracted by all the lovely, shiny objects in my midst.

It's also helpful to consider what percentage of time you spend doing things that you want to do versus those that you don't want to do, and how much time you spend doing things you have to do versus things you don't have to do. If most of your time is spent on things you don't want to do, then it's time to reconsider your role. And if you spend most of your time doing things you don't need to do, perhaps you should reconsider your priorities. The sweet spot is doing the things you both need and want to do. Of course, we often do things we don't want to do because they need to get done or because they will lead to long-term benefits. But it's worth evaluating how you spend your time, optimizing for both the short and long term.

Limiting yourself to a few core priorities can feel frustrating; however, it can help you avoid the Tyranny of the *Or*—that is, having to choose between this *or* that. For example, when you face a massive deadline everything else falls to the side. However, there are many ways to satisfy more than one desire at once. For instance, if you love to cook and want to spend time with friends, you can start a cooking club. I met a woman who had a group called Chop and Chat. Every Sunday six women would get together to cook at a member's home. Each member brought the ingredients to make a different recipe that was then split into six large portions. Members took home six different main courses for the week. Chop and Chat was an inventive way for the women to cook together, socialize, and prepare meals for their families.

You, too, can find innovative ways to combine your work and other activities about which you feel passionate. Take venture capitalist Fern Mandelbaum, for example. You would assume that meetings with Fern would take place in her office. But Fern is also an avid athlete and loves being outside, so when you want to discuss a new venture with her, be prepared to join her for a strenuous hike. Everyone who knows Fern knows to wear walking shoes and carry a bottle of water to a meeting with her. She finds that this strategy is a great way to really get to know each entrepreneur while also getting fresh air and exercise.

To summarize, with a little practice it's easy to squeeze a little more sweet juice out of every day. Always show appreciation to those who help you. Keep a stack of thank-you notes on your desk and use them frequently. Also, never forget that the world is very small and you will likely bump into the same people time and time again. Protect and enhance your reputation— it's your most valuable asset and should be guarded well. Learn how to apologize with a simple "I'm sorry." Do the right thing, as opposed to the smart thing, so you'll be proud to tell your story later. And don't take on too much, lest you disappoint yourself and those who count on you. Consider how much time you spend doing things you need and want to do, and prioritize for yourself, so someone else doesn't do it for you.

Chapter 10

Paint the Target Around the Arrow

Several years ago, when he was in high school, my son, Josh, wanted to purchase a new bicycle. He was interested in competing as a road cyclist and "needed" a fancy new bike. He came to my husband, Mike, and me and said, "I've done all my research and have found the perfect bike. It's really important to me." Our response was, "That's nice. There's no way we're going to spend that much money on a bike. We might be willing to spend half that amount." I followed with, "Look around you, Josh. Perhaps you can find a way to make purchasing the bike more attractive to us?" I urged him to think of things he could do that would be worth the price of the bike.

Josh thought for a few days and came back to us with a proposal, offering to do all of his own laundry and to cook dinner for the family three nights a week. Interesting idea . . . Mike and I took this under consideration and decided it was a good deal. By doing his laundry and making dinner, Josh would save us a lot of time, and he would learn some important skills. We agreed to the deal. Josh got the bike and took his new responsibilities seriously, building trust that we all would follow through with our promises.

Like all parents, we've had many other opportunities to negotiate future deals, which reinforces the fact that the most important outcome of any negotiation is to get to the next negotiation. The first deal is just the beginning. If the first negotiation is fair and balanced, and both parties follow through on their commitments, then chances are the next negotiation will go even more smoothly. As mentioned several times, we live in a very small world, and repeat appearances are the norm.

Most of our interactions with others are essentially a series of negotiations, and we do ourselves a huge disservice by not knowing the basic tenets. We negotiate with our friends about what to do on Saturday night, we negotiate with our family about who does the dishes and who pays the bills, we negotiate with our colleagues about who will stay late to complete an assignment, and we negotiate with salespeople on the price of a car. We negotiate all day. Most of us don't even realize we're negotiating; nor do we have any idea how to do it well. Here are some clues, learned through a classroom activity:

On the surface the following exercise appears to be a simple negotiation between job candidates and employers.[1] There are eight terms to nail down, including salary, vacation time, and job assignment, and each person has point values associated with each of the terms. Each individual's goal is to maximize his or her own points. Usually, the pairs of negotiators go down the list in order, trying to agree on each item. They quickly realize, however, that this strategy isn't going to work. At the end of a thirty-minute negotiation, some of the negotiators have come to a resolution and others have decided to walk away without a deal. The pairs who have reached an agreement fall into one of two categories: those who are eager to work together and those who feel quite uncomfortable with the outcome. Some pairs end up with similar point totals at the end, while others have wildly different scores. So what happened?

The most common mistake in all negotiations is making assumptions, and the most common assumption in this case is that the recruiter and the candidate have opposing objectives. The candidate assumes the recruiter wants the exact opposite of everything the candidate wants, when in actuality they have two of eight objectives in common, two that are opposing, two that are much more important to the candidate, and two that are much more important to the recruiter. Though contrived, this case mirrors most situations in life. Parties often share interests, even when they believe they're on opposite sides of an issue, and some terms are almost always much more important to one person than to the other.

The key to a successful negotiation is to ferret out everyone's interests so the outcome can be maximized for everyone. This is easier said than done, since most people hold their interests close to the vest, believing this gives them a stronger negotiating position. But oftentimes this strategy is misguided, because in actuality what one party wants might be right in line with what the other party wants.

Maggie Neale, an expert on negotiation, says that everyone should look at the process as a creative problem-solving exercise.[2] With that mindset you are more likely to squeeze more options out of the negotiation. I've taken this to heart. During a recent experience purchasing a car, I decided to see what would happen if I looked at the encounter through the lens of learning, and by challenging my long-held assumption that the salesperson wanted me to spend as much money as possible, because I wanted to spend as little as possible.

While test-driving the car, I amped up my curiosity and asked a lot of questions about the automobile industry, including how salespeople are compensated. I surprisingly learned that this salesperson's commission had nothing to do with the price I paid for the car. His bonus was based on getting an excellent evaluation on his customer service. I told him that wasn't a problem for me and that I'd be delighted to give him a fabulous review in return for a great price. We found a win-win situation. I would never have known or imagined that our interests were aligned if I had not taken the time to explore them.

The good news is that you get opportunities to negotiate every day and so have many chances to practice this skill. Here's a story illustrating that negotiations can happen anywhere. A few years ago I was in Beijing for a conference, and my colleague Ed Rubesch met up with some of his students from Thammasat University in Thailand who were planning a sunrise trip to the Great Wall. That sounded fantastic, and I became intent on finding a way to see the Great Wall at sunrise, too. I thought such a trip would be easy to arrange, but for some reason it turned out to be nearly impossible. I started with the concierge at the hotel, then a local professor, and then the taxi drivers near my hotel. No one was able to help me with my quest. At the same time, I was talking up this idea with other colleagues, many of whom wanted to join the excursion. We agreed to meet in the lobby of the hotel at 3:00 a.m. for the trip to the Great Wall, and it was up to me to make it happen. I wasn't going to let them down, but I had no idea how to accomplish this. I had used up all the obvious solutions.

Across the street from my hotel was a school that taught English, and I thought that at the very least I'd be able to find someone with whom I could speak. After striking out herself when she tried calling a car service, the receptionist suggested I talk with a seventeen-year-old student who was in the lobby. I introduced myself and sat down to chat with him. My goal was to find some reason he would want to help me reach my goal. After a short time, I learned he was an accomplished student, musician, and athlete who was in the midst of applying to colleges. Eureka! I'd found the way I might be able to help him. I told him that if he would help me get to the Great Wall at sunrise, then I would write a letter of recommendation for him for college. That sounded like a great deal to him, too! With several hours of effort he solved my problem by finding a car and a driver and agreeing to come along as the translator. After that, I was only too pleased to write a letter that described his initiative, creativity, and generosity. Together we created a wonderful win-win situation. This was a gift that kept on giving, since I ended up writing letters of recommendation for him for years to come.

Stan Christensen, who teaches a course on negotiation, built his career around extracting the most value from negotiations. He recommends looking for surprises when you negotiate, because surprises indicate you've made inaccurate assumptions. He also advises picking your negotiating approach based on the interests and style of the person with whom you're negotiating, not on your own interests. Don't walk into any negotiation with a clearly defined plan, but instead listen to what's said by the other party and figure out what drives them. Doing so will help you craft a positive outcome for both sides.

There are some cases that offer no win-win solution, and it's actually better to walk away. When the interests of the different players are uncovered, and it's clear there's no intersection between their goals, then walking away is the best choice. Despite this, most students strike a deal anyway, even though it's suboptimal for both parties. Many of us hold to the mistaken assumption that any deal is better than walking away. This certainly isn't always the case, and walking away from a deal should always be considered a viable option.

The best way to know whether you should walk away from a deal is to understand your other choices, so you can accurately compare them to the deal at hand. In negotiation lingo this is called a BATNA (best alternative to a negotiated agreement). Always know your BATNA when you start to negotiate. Stan uses a case study involving Disney and a group of environmentalists to illustrate this point. Disney wanted to build a new theme park and the environmentalists were opposed. They went around and around on what Disney could do to protect the environment while still building the park. The two sides were unable to reach an agreement, and the deal fell apart. The result? The new park wasn't built. However, shortly thereafter, the land was sold to a developer, who built tract housing on the same spot. The impact of the housing was much worse than the theme park's impact would have been. Had the environmentalists taken their BATNA—or possible alternative— into account, they would have realized that reaching a deal with Disney was the preferred outcome.

This happens in our everyday lives, too. If we don't fully appreciate our alternatives, we may make a big mistake. For example, you may walk away from a job offer that isn't perfect only to find that you are unemployed, or stick with a relationship that isn't optimal because you didn't realize that you actually had much better opportunities elsewhere.

In general, to negotiate effectively you need to understand your own goals as well as the goals of the other party, attempt to come up with a win-win outcome, and know when to walk away. It sounds simple, but it takes a lot of effort to master these skills and to ensure that both parties are satisfied.

●   ●   ●

Getting out of your own head and seeing other people's perspectives is critical well beyond negotiations. It is important to make all relationships work, to make teams work, and to make yourself successful. With increased empathy, it becomes clear that most people are struggling with something. Some of those struggles are easily visible, like a broken leg or a black eye, while most reside deep below the surface. I love the lyrics from a Red Hot Chili Peppers song: "Scar tissue that I wish you saw." This line reminds me that we never really know what's going on with someone else.

In fact, our own pains and disappointments are a gateway to understanding and appreciating the pains and disappointments of others, and a reminder that we should treat everyone as if they have a "broken heart" because they probably do. Yes, each challenge we face presents us with the opportunity to develop tools for coping with similar challenges in the future. But it also provides an opportunity to experience and appreciate the world from others' perspectives.

Unfortunately, in school most of us spend so much time in situations in which we're encouraged to win at someone else's expense that it's hard to get practice helping others. I remember my first week of college, when I asked a girl in my dorm to help me with a calculus assignment. Without skipping a beat, she said, "If I help you, then you will do better than I will and you'll get into medical school and I won't." I'm not exaggerating. She wasn't willing to help me because we might be competing four years in the future. Years later, I listened to my son lament that all of his classes were graded on a curve. This meant that in addition to focusing on learning the material for an exam, he and his classmates had to think about how well they would perform relative to one another. This is a huge disincentive to helping others.

After years of learning in such an environment, I had no idea how to be a good team player. It took me a long time to realize that this competitive mindset, in which you win at someone else's expense, is completely counterproductive. Almost everything in life is done in teams, and those who don't know how to make others successful are at a huge disadvantage. The best team players go to great lengths to make others successful. In fact, the higher you reach within an organization, the less important your individual contributions become. Instead, your job becomes leading, inspiring, and motivating others. Most of your work is done by colleagues tasked with implementing your ideas. Therefore, if you can't work well with others, then your ability to execute diminishes. Successful team players understand what drives each person on the team and look for ways to make them successful. Additionally, great leaders figure out a way for everyone to play to his or her individual strengths.

I've been on teams in which everyone on the team feels as though he or she got the "easy" job. If you think about it, this is the perfect work environment. Each person is doing what he or she does best and is extremely appreciative of what the other people on the team bring to the table. Everyone has a job perfectly tuned to their skills and interests. Each person feels great about their contributions and celebrates the contributions of others. The saying "Paint the target around the arrow" summarizes this wonderfully. I first heard this from my colleague Forrest Glick. It had been a mantra in his group when he worked at Harvard University. The idea is that you should pick the most talented person you can (*the arrow*) and then craft the job (*the target*) around what he or she does best. If you allow really talented people to do what they do best, then the results are astonishing. They're fulfilled and, therefore, much more productive than if they were doing something that didn't fit their talents or interests. The key is putting together a team with the right complement of skills.

No matter where you are, you are very likely to need help from others to succeed. This includes help finding information, resources, contacts, and opportunities. Knowing how to ask for help is pivotal. If you ask properly, you are much more likely to get a positive response, and if you ask poorly, you probably won't get a response. Heidi Roizen is incredibly generous in helping others and says that the way others ask determines the type of response they get from her. For example, she tells our students that when people ask her for a favor, they often optimize their own time and put more of the burden on her. They may send her a rambling email that she will have to parse to figure out what they want, and then cut it apart to send to different people. Instead, she suggests doing your homework. If Heidi has offered to introduce you to several people, then create a set of customized messages that she can easily forward with a short introduction. If you make it easy for her to help you, she will do it quickly. If you make it hard for her, she says, your request will drop to the bottom of her stack.[3] Essentially, make it easy for others to help you. Look at the situation from their perspective, and figure out how to make the ask as simple as possible.

We live in a complex world and are deeply dependent upon others. Therefore, it is critically important to know how to work well with others, optimize your negotiations, extract the most from your teams, and make yourself easy to help. Each of these skills propels you forward while also helping those around you reach their objectives.

Chapter 11

Will This Be on the Exam?

I never use slides in my class, except on the first day, when I describe what we'll cover over the ten-week quarter. The final slide always lists my commitments to the class and what I expect of the students. The last point is "Never miss an opportunity to be fabulous." I promise to deliver my very best in each class and expect the same from them. I also tell the students that I have no problem giving everyone an A, but that the bar is set very high. This is the first and last time I mention this.

So what happens? The students consistently deliver more than I or they ever imagined. They embrace the idea of being fabulous with remarkable enthusiasm and raise the bar repeatedly as the quarter progresses. In fact, several years ago I arrived at class a few minutes early and found one of my students sitting outside listening to her new iPod Nano. I hadn't seen one before and asked to take a look. She handed it to me and turned it over. The back was engraved with the words "Never miss an opportunity to be fabulous!" Apparently, when she ordered it online, she had the option of having it engraved. Instead of adding her name or contact information, she chose this message, which she wanted to remember every day. She certainly didn't do this for me; she did it for herself.

I'm no longer surprised by the stickiness of this message. I now know that everyone is just waiting to get this instruction. They're hungry for permission to do their very best, to hit the ball out of the park, and to shine their brightest. Unfortunately, in most situations this doesn't happen. We're encouraged to "satisfice." That is, we're subtly or not so subtly encouraged to do the least amount we can to satisfy the requirements. For example, teachers give assignments and clearly state what's required to get specific grades. And the classic question posed to a teacher is "Will this be on the exam?" Students have learned through years of reinforcement that all they need to do is meet the minimum requirement to get the grade they want. This happens at work as well, when bosses outline specific objectives for their staff and create rubrics and metrics for giving bonuses and promotions.

It's easy to meet expectations, knowing exactly what you will get in return. But amazing things happen when you remove the cap. In fact, I believe there's a huge pent-up drive in each of us to blow off the cap. Like a soda bottle that's been shaken, individuals who remove perceived limits achieve remarkable results.

There are some people who always deliver their best, even in very challenging situations. Consider Ashwini Doshi, whom I first met about fifteen years ago when, as a graduate student, she applied for a research assistant job in our department. Despite my openness, I was really taken aback when she walked into my office for the job interview. Ashwini was a beautiful woman, and she was only three and a half feet tall. Her voice was that of a little girl, but her ideas were those of a mature adult. I'm embarrassed to say that I didn't hire her for the position. This happened to Ashwini a lot. People were so surprised by her appearance that it usually took several interactions before they were comfortable enough to see past her physical differences. I'm fortunate that she decided to take my course, because it gave me an opportunity to get to know her quite well. When another position became available in our group, I jumped at the chance to hire her. Ashwini's work was exemplary, she was a terrific team player, and she always went way beyond what was expected.

Born in Mumbai (formerly Bombay), Ashwini grew up in a household of nineteen—her father, his three brothers, their wives, all of their children, and her grandparents. She was born normal size, but by the time she was a year old, it was clear that she wasn't growing properly. The doctors in India weren't able to provide guidance on her care, so her parents sent X-rays of her tiny skeleton to specialists in the United States. The only medical option was to put bone extensions in each of her extremities, a process that would have required extensive surgery over six years. She also would have been bedridden for months at a time, which was out of the question for this very active young girl.

Ashwini was fortunate that her family was so open-minded and loving. In many families, someone so different would have caused great embarrassment and, so, been hidden away. But they didn't do this to Ashwini. In fact, she went to the best schools in Bombay and always excelled. She had a remarkably positive attitude, and from a young age felt strangely empowered by her differences. Ashwini thought of herself as a normal person living an extraordinary life.

Ashwini sincerely felt that there was nothing she couldn't do and demonstrated this time and again. She came to California all by herself to attend graduate school. In addition to the cultural differences and her physical limitations, she didn't know anyone when she arrived. Many of her friends in India encouraged her to stay put, saying life would be much easier for her there. But she persisted. Once she arrived at Stanford, the only accommodation she received was a small step stool in her apartment that would enable her to reach the stove. Out of necessity, she figured out ingenious solutions to all the physical obstacles she faced every single day.

When I asked Ashwini about the problems she encountered, she had a hard time coming up with any. She just didn't see them. When pressed, she cited the difficulty of finding a driving school willing to accept her as a student. After years of depending on rides from friends and on public transportation, she decided to learn to drive and purchased a set of pedal extenders so she could reach the gas and brake pedals. It took dozens of calls before she found a driving school that would take her.

What is most impressive is that Ashwini always delivered more than 100 percent of what she was called upon to do. Her only regret? She actually wished she had taken even more risks when she was younger. Despite all she had overcome, Ashwini thought she had taken the safe path. She embraced the idea that life isn't a dress rehearsal and that you get only one chance to do the best job. Sadly, she died earlier this year due to complications from surgery. Her memory lives on as a powerful reminder to never miss an opportunity to be fabulous.

Being fabulous implies making the decision to go beyond what's expected. The benefits for this are enormous. On the flip side, if you do less than is expected, then the collection of missed opportunities adds up, leading to a huge deficit.

I discussed this observation with Steve Garrity, a former student and successful entrepreneur. He couldn't agree more. In fact, he shared how he communicates this to his team. Steve tells his colleagues that every day they each make tiny choices. If they choose wisely, then, just like adding money to an investment account, the effects of these small changes are compounded, yielding tremendous results over time.[1]

Consider the difference between someone who does just their assigned job versus someone who does only 1 percent better each day. If your job is defined by a value of 1.0, and that is all you do, then:

$1.0 \times 1.0 \times 1.0 \ldots (365 \text{ times}) = 1.0$
Nothing changes for you.

If you do only 1 percent better each day, then:
$1.01 \times 1.01 \times 1.01 \ldots (365 \text{ times}) = 37.78$

Wow!

In the beginning a 1 percent improvement is imperceptible. After seven days, the result is only 1.07. It isn't until this pattern of improvement is in place for seventy days (a little over two months) that you get to 2.0 times better. And at seven hundred days (less than two years), you are over a thousand times better than when you started.

If, on the other hand, you do 1 percent worse each day, at the end of the year the result is a tiny 0.02. Therefore, in one year, the difference between someone who does 1 percent better and 1 percent worse each day is almost two thousand times!

This happens in all aspects of our lives. Kevin Weil, former head of product at Instagram, provided a great analogy. He is an ultramarathon runner, which means he frequently runs fifty miles at a time. When I asked him how running influences his work, he reflected on the fact that over the course of a week of training it is rare to see any major improvement in his pace, even though he gets a little better each day. However, after a year, it is clearly evident that he has made significant strides in his performance. He applies this to his work, too, knowing that each day that he pushes himself just a little further amounts in meaningful long-term results. Essentially, you get out of life what you put in, and the results are compounded daily.[2]

•   •   •

Bernie Roth, a Stanford mechanical engineering professor, does a provocative exercise at the d.school to highlight this point. He selects a student to come up to the front of the room and says, "*Try* to take this empty water bottle out of my hand." Bernie holds the bottle tightly and the student tries, and inevitably fails, to take it. Bernie then changes the phrasing slightly, saying, "*Take* the water bottle from my hand." The student then makes a bigger effort, usually without result. Prodding the student further, Bernie insists that the student *take* the bottle from him. Usually the student succeeds on the third attempt. The lesson? There's a big difference between trying to do something and actually doing it. We often say we're trying to do something—lose weight, get more exercise, find a job.

But the truth is, we're either doing it or not doing it. Trying to do it is a cop-out. You have to focus your intention to make something happen by giving at least 100 percent commitment. Anything less and you're the only one to blame for failing to reach your goals. As Yoda in the famous Star Wars film *The Empire Strikes Back* says, "Do. Or do not. There is no try."

Bernie also tells students that excuses are irrelevant or, to use the technical term, bullshit. We use excuses to cover up the fact that we didn't put in the required effort to deliver. This lesson is relevant in all parts of life. There's no excuse for being late, for not handing in an assignment, for failing an exam, for not spending time with your family, for not calling your girlfriend, and so forth. You can manufacture an excuse that's socially acceptable, such as having too much work or being sick, but if you really wanted to deliver, you'd figure out a way to make it happen.

These are harsh words, since we're all so used to generating and hearing excuses. Bernie acknowledges that making excuses, or giving reasons for not delivering, is socially acceptable because it makes you sound "reasonable." But even if you feel obliged to make excuses to others, you shouldn't make them to yourself. You need to come to terms with the fact that if you really want to accomplish something, it's up to you to do so. Make it a high priority or drop it from your list. To drive home this point, Bernie asks his students to write down their biggest goal and then to list every impediment that prevents them from reaching it. It typically takes several minutes to compose the list. He then challenges the students to see that the only item that should be on the list is their own name. We make excuses for not reaching our goals by blaming others and external factors for getting in the way or for not enabling us. Again, achieving is your responsibility from start to finish. These exercises, and the lessons they deliver, reinforce the notion that we are each ultimately in charge of our own lives. There is no excuse for delivering anything short of one's best effort.

This isn't just true for individuals. It is also true for organizations. Chip and Dan Heath describe this in depth in their book *The Power of Moments*. I had a chance to interview Chip as part of our Entrepreneurial Thought Leaders lecture series, during which he shared examples of companies creating remarkable experiences. Their framework describes how shifts in the way we act—at work, with our family, on vacation, etc.—have a huge impact when those acts amplify moments of elevation, pride, insight, and connection to others. One of my favorite examples is about how John Deere, the tractor manufacturer, designs the first day on the job in order to make it an incredibly meaningful moment for new employees.

Chip explains that the typical first day of a new job involves the following scenario: You show up, and the person at the reception desk is really happy to see you but thought you were coming in next week. The monitor for your computer is there, but the CPU isn't hooked up. The person you are scheduled to meet is late, so they grab an employee manual that is sitting in the cubicle from the last owner and tell you to look through it for a while. So, you spend your morning reading expense reimbursement policy and assorted other technical things. Finally, right before lunch, somebody takes pity on you and whisks you around the office to meet twenty-three people who are late for a meeting, and so you feel guilty for interrupting them. It's certainly not an optimal experience for a first day at work.

Does this sound familiar? He goes on to describe how John Deere addresses these issues. First, they assign each new employee a texting buddy at the company to help with anything they need, from finding a room to how to dress the first day of work. When a new employee shows up the first day, someone hands them their favorite drink, whether it's a can of soda or a low-fat latte. The monitor in the reception area has their name on it, welcoming them to their first day of work at the company. In addition, there's a banner at their cubicle that allows others to see that there is a new person in the group, and they can then stop by at their leisure to say hello. A computer is set up on their desk, and their first email is in their inbox, from the CEO. He shares the company's 175-year history and its mission to help the world produce more food and shelter. He says, "Welcome to the most important work that you'll ever do, and we hope you will have a long history with John Deere."[3]

The experience goes on and on, including lunch with peers at work and the gift of a model tractor. The new employee ends the day elated, knowing that the work they are doing is important and feeling connected to those with whom they will be working. Yes, this takes thought and effort, but the payoff is huge. We can each take time to consider ways we can go beyond the expected to the exceptional in all aspects of the things we do.

●   ●   ●

Being fabulous also shifts the way you engage with others. We often assume that successful people are highly competitive and accomplished their goals at the expense of others. But this certainly isn't the case. There's a significant difference between being competitive and being driven. Being competitive implies a zero-sum game in which you succeed at someone else's expense. Being driven involves tapping into your own passion to make things happen.

I designed an exercise to highlight the point that to be successful in an entrepreneurial environment, it's often more productive to be driven than to be competitive. In the exercise I divide a group into six teams and then unveil five completed jigsaw puzzles, each with a hundred pieces.[4] Participants are allowed to see the puzzles for a minute or so, and then all the pieces from the five puzzles are dumped into a pillowcase and mixed up. All but a few pieces—which I secretly hold back and auction off later—are then randomly distributed to the six teams. Each team is also given twenty poker chips to use as currency. The teams are responsible for completing a puzzle within an hour. When the time is up, points are calculated. Each team counts the number of pieces in the largest completed section of the puzzle and receives one point for each piece. They then count the number of pieces in small islands of connected pieces and receive half a point for each piece. Each team that completes an entire jigsaw puzzle in an hour earns a twenty-five-point bonus.

Since there are fewer puzzles than there are teams, participants have to decide if they're going to compete, collaborate, or both to collect the necessary puzzle pieces. This situation is meant to mimic the real world: participants know all the pieces exist to complete the task, but no one team controls them all. Teams have to find ways to get the resources they need to be successful. Additionally, since there aren't enough puzzles for every team, some teams have to find an alternative way to create value. As in the real world, there are many different roles to be played within an ecosystem. Also, the world is not static. After the game begins, every ten minutes or so something happens. I sell photos of the completed puzzles, require one person from each team to move to another team, taking a few puzzle pieces with him or her, and auction off the remaining puzzle pieces. The changing environment requires both creativity and flexibility.

In order to be successful, the teams must work together. They start the game by trading and bartering, trying to figure out how to maximize their own benefits without giving away too much. This requires balancing strategy with action, figuring out how to divide the labor among team members and how to walk the line between competition and collaboration, all in an ever-changing environment. Since they know there are fewer puzzles than there are teams, at least one team has to decide to *not* build a puzzle and to instead take on a different role. Sometimes one team chooses to divide up and join other teams. Sometimes two or three teams merge. At other times a team may take on the role of broker, buying and selling puzzle pieces from the other teams. And sometimes all of the teams merge into one huge team and work on all of the puzzles together. I like to do this exercise with larger groups that I can divide into two or more ecosystems, each with six teams and five puzzles. Doing so allows different strategies to evolve in parallel, which makes for interesting comparisons afterward.

The very worst outcome results when all of the teams decide to compete against one another. They hold back puzzle pieces and refuse to trade pieces needed by other teams. These groups become so focused on winning that they all lose. Some teams acknowledge that they knew they would have done better if they had collaborated but decided to compete anyway.

Competition is so built into our culture that it becomes the natural response. Additionally, those teams that work hard to make other teams lose end up losing themselves. For example, the first time I ran this simulation, one team decided to hold on to a handful of pieces that other teams needed. Toward the end of the hour they planned to sell them to the other teams. This backfired. When the time was up, the teams had spent so much time competing with one another that they weren't even close to completing a puzzle. This meant the final pieces didn't offer any additional value.

This exercise offers a strong reminder that in environments where there are limited resources, being driven to make yourself and others successful is often a much more productive strategy than being purely competitive. Those who do this are better able to leverage the skills and tools that others bring to the table, and to celebrate other people's successes along with their own. This happens in sports as well as in business settings, which are both often thought to be purely competitive environments. For example, competitors in the Tour de France work together over the course of the twenty-one-day race in order to make everyone successful. They know that in order to continue racing in the future with professional endorsements, riders need to win at least one stage of the race. Therefore, they let different riders win over the course of the race, providing them with the credibility they need to continue riding. Similarly, many competitive companies embrace the concept of "coopetition" by finding creative ways to work together, leveraging each business's strengths and letting them each win.

When it comes to being fabulous, many businesses select one area in which they really shine. BMW focuses on top-notch engineering, Walmart promises the lowest prices, Disneyland strives to be the happiest place on earth, and Nordstrom works hard to deliver a world-class customer experience. If you ask people familiar with the store what they think about Nordstrom, most will offer at least one story about the incredible service they received.

I had an opportunity to meet with two of the three Nordstrom brothers, Erik and Blake, and learned how they instill their employees with customer-centric values. Surprisingly, there are no specific rules or secret recipes for providing an outstanding customer experience at Nordstrom. Essentially, after only a short orientation, salespeople are charged with using their best judgment in solving the problems that come their way and are empowered to act on their customers' behalf. Because each salesperson is different, they deal with their customers in unique ways, leading to a wide array of approaches to similar challenges. There's also a culture of telling stories at Nordstrom, and great customer-service stories serve as lessons and inspiration. By empowering employees to be inventive in solving problems, Nordstrom also gives them the freedom to make mistakes. Blake and Erik both pointed out that if an error is made in an effort to serve the customer, it's quickly forgiven—and the same mistake is rarely repeated.

At Nordstrom, all incentives are aligned to create a terrific customer experience. Each manager works to make his or her

own team successful, and all employees view their customers as the ultimate "boss." The senior managers of the company spend half their time visiting stores, where they walk the
sales floor, interact with customers, and talk with the sales
personnel—including the Nordstrom brothers. They were very
familiar with this environment, each having started his career
working in the Nordstrom stockroom, selling shoes, managing shoe departments, serving as buyers, managing individual
stores, and then acting as regional managers. As leaders of
this multibillion-dollar business, they have always been looking for ways to improve. They watched and listened carefully,
with great humility, and then, based on the information they
gathered, acted with confidence and conviction. So intent on
continuing to enhance customer satisfaction, they made it remarkably easy for any customer to reach each of them. They
have always answered their own phones, read their own email,
and responded to messages personally.

The idea that the customer comes first is so embedded in
the culture of Nordstrom that the brothers described the organization as an upside-down pyramid, with the customer at
the top and the senior management at the bottom. When an
employee advances in the company, he or she literally moves
down the corporate ladder. There's also no chief executive officer at the bottom. They work as a very tight team, each brother
playing to his own strengths. They share a vision for the business and work in a concerted and collaborative manner.

My favorite customer-service story from Nordstrom is of a
customer who asked the men's department for two blue button-
down shirts with white collars. The salesperson helping him
couldn't find these in stock or at any of the other Nordstrom

stores. But instead of telling the customer they couldn't meet his request, she took two white shirts and two blue shirts to the store tailor and asked to have the collars switched so there were two blue shirts with white collars and two white shirts with blue collars. She presented the blue shirts to the customer and told him that if he wanted the reverse, that was now available, too!

When we met, both Blake and Erik pointed out that every experience with each customer is like a fresh chance at bat. Each interaction is another opportunity to deliver a great experience for the customer and to enhance the salesperson's reputation. Even if their actions don't lead to a specific sale, the investment eventually pays off.

Being fabulous comes in many flavors, but it all starts with removing the cap and being willing to reach for your true potential. This means going beyond minimum expectations and acknowledging that you are ultimately responsible for your actions and the resulting outcomes. Doing just 1 percent better each day leads to enormous positive results. Life isn't a dress rehearsal, and you won't always get a second chance to do your best.

Chapter 12

Experimental Artifacts

I have a confession to make—I easily could have titled all of the previous chapters "Give Yourself Permission." By that I mean, give yourself permission to challenge assumptions, to look at the world with fresh eyes, to experiment, to fail, to plot your own course, and to test the limits of your abilities. In fact, that's exactly what I wish I had known when I was twenty, and thirty, and forty—and what I need to constantly remind myself at sixty.

It's incredibly easy to get locked into traditional ways of thinking and to block out possible alternatives. For most of us, there are crowds of people standing on the sidelines, encouraging each of us to stay on the prescribed path, to color inside the lines, and to follow the same directions they followed. This is comforting to them and might be for you. It reinforces the choices they made and provides you with a recipe that's easy to follow. But it can also be severely limiting.

Not only do others feel comforted if you follow their path, but they are sometimes relieved that you are not surpassing them. In Latin America there is actually a phrase that translates into "jacket puller" to describe people who try to pull others down—presumably by the tails of their jackets—to prevent others from rising higher than they have. People in other parts of the world call this the "tall poppy" syndrome, in which those who stand up taller than the people around them are cut down to size. Staying with the pack is the norm, and those who get ahead risk being dragged backward by their community. Worse still, there are also regions of the world where those who do things differently are literally viewed as criminals. In Brazil, for instance, the traditional word for "entrepreneur," *empresário*, translates loosely into "thief." Historically, there are not many local role models for successful entrepreneurs, and others assume you've done something illegal if you've successfully broken the mold.

This was a significant problem for Endeavor, the organization whose goal is to enhance entrepreneurship in the developing world. When they launched in Latin America, Endeavor told people they wanted to stimulate entrepreneurship, and they were met with great resistance. In response, they literally coined a brand-new word, *emprendedor,* to capture the true essence of innovation and entrepreneurial spirit. It took several years, but eventually *emprendedor* entered the lexicon. Endeavor faced a similar challenge in Egypt, where they needed to create and promote a new word for entrepreneur.

Within our programs at Stanford much of our work focuses on giving students permission to challenge assumptions and to stretch their imaginations by breaking free from traditional ways of thinking. Most assignments my colleagues and I give in our classes require students to leave their comfort zones and engage anew with the world around them. The faculty poses the challenges, but we don't have the answers.

Additionally, at the Stanford d.school our classroom space invites experimentation. All of the furniture is on wheels and moves about easily to create different workspaces. Each time students arrive, the space is configured differently. Bins of paper, wood, plastic, paper clips, rubber bands, colored pens, pipe cleaners, and tape encourage them to build prototypes to bring their ideas to life. The rooms are filled with movable whiteboards covered with colored stickies for brainstorming. The walls are peppered with photos and artifacts from past projects that serve as inspiration for creative thinking.

Our students are given real, open-ended challenges. For example, they might be asked to figure out how to improve bike safety on campus or to find a way to entice kids to eat healthier food. Besides these local projects, d.school students in the Design for Extreme Affordability class work with partners in developing countries to identify problems and determine how to solve them in cost-effective ways. This project has led to a number of exciting products that are now on the market. For example, one team designed a brand-new baby incubator, Embrace, after visiting hospitals in Nepal and finding that traditional Western baby incubators, whose original price tag was $20,000, were not well suited to the local environment. Many were broken or in need of unavailable parts. The operating instructions and warning labels were in a language foreign to the nursing staff. Most important, the majority of births occur in villages far from city hospitals with incubators. Therefore, premature babies who need to be kept warm with an incubator rarely get access to the help they need.

The team identified the need for a low-cost, low-technology incubator that could be used outside a hospital. Over the course of a few months they designed a tiny sleeping bag with a pouch-insert containing a special wax. The melting temperature of the wax is 37 degrees centigrade, the temperature needed to keep a newborn baby warm.[1] For just $20, as opposed to $20,000, parents or local clinics can now take care of a premature baby on-site, in transit, or at home. They remove the insert and place it in hot water to melt the wax. The insert is then put into the insulated sleeping bag, where it stays warm for hours. When it eventually cools down, the wax can easily be warmed up again. No technical training is needed, no electricity is required, and the design is inexpensive enough to be deployed in underserved communities without access to urban hospitals.

The students leave these courses changed forever. They have a new appreciation for the power of paying attention to the problems in the world around them, and they learn that they're empowered to fix them. As David Kelley, the founding director of the d.school, would say, "They are leaving with creative confidence."[2] They know they have permission—both explicit and implicit—to experiment, to fail, and to try again. What we must all recognize is that every one of us has the same permission—we just need to recognize that it's ours to grant ourselves and not something extended from outside.

It's important to remember that we are each responsible for crafting our own personal story, and for understanding how our story both empowers and limits us. This message was driven home to me in an unexpected way. A few years ago I took a creative writing class in which the professor asked us to describe the same scene twice, the first time from the perspective of someone who has just fallen in love, the second from the point of view of someone who has just lost a child to war. We were not allowed to mention falling in love or the war. This simple assignment revealed how completely different the world looks depending on our emotional state. When I imagined walking through a crowded city in a state of bliss, my mind was focused on the colors and sounds, and my view was expansive. When strolling through a similar scene in a depressed state, everything looked gray, and all the imperfections, such as cracks in the sidewalk, jumped into focus. I couldn't see beyond my own feet, and the city seemed daunting, as opposed to stimulating. I dug up what I wrote for that assignment:

> Sarah leaned over to admire the bouquet of peach-colored roses she had just bought. Her mind wandered fancifully from the flowers to the wonderful smell of fresh bread coming from the bakery next door. Standing to the side of the entrance was an amateur juggler. With his wildly colored costume, he attracted an audience of children who giggled each time he made a mistake. She watched a few minutes and found herself giggling too. He finished his performance with a foppish bow toward Sarah. She took a deep bow in return and handed him a rose.

●   ●   ●

> Joe walked with his head down, protecting himself from the icy fog, as wind-whipped newspapers sailed

through the air, slapping against the buildings before taking off again. "Step on a crack, break your mother's back. Step on a line, break your mother's spine." These words kept running through Joe's mind as he passed each crack that disrupted the rhythmic pattern of the sidewalk. The childhood taunt became a low drone in the back of his brain as he focused on the uneven path that stretched in front of him.

This was a valuable assignment not just for practicing my writing skills but for life in general, a poignant reminder that we choose how we view the world around us. The environment is filled with flaws and flowers, and we each decide which to embrace. Our perception becomes our reality.

I recently had a chance to attend the Modern Elder Academy in Baja, Mexico, run by Chip Conley.[3] The goal of the program is to provide a framework for rethinking our roles in the world later in life. There was a recurring reference to the "liminal state," meaning threshold, where you are moving between two roles, like a caterpillar turning into a butterfly. We were reminded that while in its cocoon, a caterpillar literally turns into soup, with only a few "imaginal discs" intact. The caterpillar essentially reinvents itself by recycling all the original material while keeping a core of what it was before.

The experiences over the week were designed to help each person shed the things that were no longer useful to them and to build upon those that are. By doing this as a group, in a concentrated time, we got to witness each person's liminal state. It was both fascinating and instructive to watch all of the transitions, some of which were clearly very hard. I wish we had taken a before-and-after photo of the group because the internal changes were matched by dramatic physical transformations as each person unfolded into the person they wanted to be. While there, I wrote a number of poems to capture the experience. The one below was about how something as simple as sand can be viewed so differently depending upon one's perspective.

Sand

Beaten, Battered, Broken
Seasoned, Salted, Spent
Trodden, Tainted, Tattered
Withered, Woken, Went

Grounded, Gentle, Guided
Settled, Sagely, Sweet
Reflective, Rhythms, Reset
Collective, Calm, Complete

● ● ●

We are deeply influenced by the stories others tell us and those we tell ourselves, and these stories shape the possibilities we see in our future. In fact, we aren't only influenced by our own personal experiences but also by our ancestors' experiences. There is evidence for transgenerational trauma carried by the descendants of Holocaust survivors, American Indians, and African Americans whose relatives were enslaved, as well as those who have been subjected to severe poverty or loss. Most of us are told stories about past generations, with clear lessons attached. And our parents' and grandparents' experiences change the way they treat their offspring. Sometimes the stories and lessons are of good fortune, and sometimes they transfer severe stress to the next generation.

In order to shape your own story, you need to understand who and where you are now, how you got here, your strengths and weaknesses, and where you want to go from here. You need to understand what holds you back, what pushes you forward, and what you're bringing along with you on your journey. You need to interpret what others told you about your past and what you tell yourself about your future.

I was recently at an event where there were lots of young children, ranging from six months to six years of age. It was fascinating to see how different they were from one another. There were children who were quick to smile, those with pensive gazes, those who always looked sad, those who always jumped up to participate, and those who stood back, watching carefully from the sidelines. It was clear that from this early age they already had a story—verbal and nonverbal—about their place in the world. Their personal stories appeared to begin long before they were born.

Shirzad Chamine has done a lot of work unpacking the types of stories we tell ourselves about who we are, and how those stories help or hinder us. In his book *Positive Intelligence*, Shirzad describes ten different "saboteurs," as well as a "sage," that shape how we engage with the world. The saboteurs include the judge, stickler, pleaser, hyper-vigilant, restless, controller, avoider, hyper-achiever, victim, and hyper-rational.[4] Understanding how these voices in our head influence how we view each situation provides some guidance on how to quiet them.

As a hyper-vigilant, I know that voice well. It is always telling me about the things that could go wrong and the dangers ahead. As Shirzad says, "The constant anxiety burns a great deal of vital energy that could otherwise be put to great use." Although being vigilant is helpful in some situations, when it kicks into high gear, it is counterproductive and destructive.

This is true of all the other saboteurs Shirzad describes. For example, avoiders try to escape conflict by saying yes to things they shouldn't and downplay real problems. Hyper-achievers are highly focused on how others see them, leading to "unsustainable workaholic tendencies." And controllers need to feel in charge of a situation and often push others beyond their comfort zone.

Shirzad came to our creativity class and ran an exercise with the students showing them how to recognize their own saboteurs and how to calm those voices by doing exercises that redirect their attention. Most important, the students were comforted to know that we all have these voices and to learn about their teammates' saboteurs. It helped them interpret one another's behavior and gave them tools for working together more effectively, including by identifying a saboteur when it shows up.

Essentially, what we achieve is influenced by where we have been and what we tell ourselves. For example, consider how each of the following four people—each of whom has nothing—would engage with the world around them given their different backgrounds:

- Someone who never had anything
- Someone who grew up in comfort and then lost it all
- Someone who started with nothing, built a comfortable life, and then lost it
- Someone who grew up with abundance, has nothing now, and knows it will be there later

Although today they are all in the same place—with nothing—they come to that place from very different experiences. As a result, they see and seize very different opportunities. Which one will be more comfortable taking risks? Which one will hold back for fear of failure? Which one will see possibilities that others don't? And which one will be hungry to do something big? This clearly depends on the story they tell themselves about their current situation and their prospects for the future.

Your current position may look the same to the outside world. However, your past experiences color the possibilities you see in front of you. Last year I experienced this in a very powerful way. I took a group of fifteen Stanford students to South Africa for two weeks to learn about innovation in this developing economy. We spent very little time together before the trip, and we all arrived in Johannesburg on the same day. Although all were Stanford students, it was clear that their past experiences had a huge impact on how they experienced the country.

Some of the students had traveled extensively before, and others hadn't. Some came from affluent families, and others came from homes of modest means. They also had grown up all over the world, from California to Jamaica to Lebanon. Therefore, they each saw South Africa—which is a complicated place with a complicated history—with different eyes. Honestly, I was not prepared for this. I mistakenly thought we would have a shared experience, but each of us had an experience that was unique, based on our past experiences. After some tricky early misunderstandings, this ultimately led to some very informative discussions about how each of us experienced the country. This continues to remind me that being in the same *position* does not mean we are actually in the same *place*.

Your position is how the world sees you, and your place is how you see yourself in the world. These are rarely the same thing, and they tend to diverge as we get older since few people actually see all the things that influenced who you are today. For example, if you were to meet Peggy Burke today, you would see a successful entrepreneur who runs a high-profile branding firm. You'd see all she has accomplished, building the company over the past thirty years, and will likely make all sorts of assumptions about her path to this position. You wouldn't know how much work went into building the business, the near-death experiences the firm faced over the years, and how Peggy's early life was riddled with financial uncertainty when her father's business failed, leaving her and her nine siblings in dire straits.

This story of losing everything when she was young is deeply embedded in Peggy's story about herself and motivates her to work incredibly hard every single day. She never takes success for granted and is driven to make sure that her business is on strong footing. Nobody sees this story when they meet Peggy. They see a positive, confident, and generous leader. Her *position* in the world as seen by others is quite different from her *place* in the world as she sees herself. As this story reminds us, where you begin is certainly not an accurate predictor of where you will end up. There are those who begin life with everything and squander those resources. There are those who start with nothing who manage to make something from nothing.

•   •   •

I shared some of the stories from this book with my father, who then decided to take some time to reflect on his most important insights, looking back over the ninety-two years of his life. Despite his currently comfortable position, his path was far from preordained. He moved to the United States when he was eight years old. His family escaped from Germany in the 1930s, and they arrived with essentially nothing. My father spoke no English, and his parents didn't have enough money to support their two children, so he lived with relatives, with whom he couldn't communicate, until his parents could afford to bring him home. From these humble beginnings, my father built an impressive life and career, and retired as executive vice president and chief operating officer at a large multinational corporation.

Reflecting on his life, my father determined that his most important insight is that you shouldn't take yourself too seriously or judge others too harshly. He wishes he had been more tolerant of mistakes he made and those made by others, and that he could have seen that failure is a normal part of the learning process. He realizes now that most of our errors are not earth-shattering, and he shared the story that brought this home for him. Working at RCA, a large US electronics company, early in his career, he and his team had a project that was going very badly. My father and his colleagues stayed up for days on end trying to fix the problems. Working to find a solution became their entire focus for weeks. Shortly after the project was successfully completed, the entire program was canceled. Even though the project was the center of their universe, to others it was expendable. He learned many times over that most things in life, especially our failures, aren't as important as we think they are at the time.

My father also reminded me that success is sweet but transient. When you're in a position of influence, authority, and power, the benefits are wonderful. But once the position is gone, the perks evaporate. Your "power" comes from the position you hold. When you're no longer in that position, all that goes with it quickly fades away. Therefore, you should not define yourself by your current position or believe all your own press. Savor the spotlight when you have it, but be ready to yield center stage when it's time to go. When you leave a job, the organization will go on without you, as you are not indispensable. Of course, you will leave a legacy of all you have accomplished, but that, too, fades with time.

Today, my father is also acutely aware of the joy of being alive. Several years ago he had a heart attack, and his implanted defibrillator is a constant reminder of his mortality. We all know intellectually that each day is precious, but as we grow older or deal with a life-threatening illness, this sentiment grows increasingly more palpable. My father works hard to make each opportunity stand out, to appreciate every moment, and to avoid squandering even a single day.

•   •   •

In looking for inspiration for this book, I literally and figuratively opened every drawer and looked into every closet of my life. In the process, I stumbled upon a canvas duffel bag I've been dragging around for forty years. The two-foot-long bag is filled with "treasures" that seemed important to me at the time. When I was twenty, this bag was one of my few possessions. I carried it with me from college to graduate school and everywhere I've lived since. Though I rarely open it, I always know where to find it. The bag and its contents are a tangible link to my past.

When I opened the bag, I found a small collection of unremarkable rocks and shells from far-off beaches, faded photo IDs dating back through my years of high school and college, a stack of old letters, and some of my early "inventions," including prototype LED jewelry that I crafted out of modeling clay and watch batteries. I also found a small notebook of poetry, titled *Experimental Artifacts*.

When I wrote the poems in the notebook they represented the flip side of the organized scientific experiments I was performing in my neuroscience lab while in graduate school. One of the poems, called "Entropy," jumped out at me. This poem was my attempt to find humor in all the uncertainty I was facing. I wrote the poem in September 1983. At that time the future was murky because I couldn't see very far into it. At the risk of embarrassing myself, I will include the poem, since many people asked to see it after the release of the first edition of this book:

Entropy

Life is like a game called Entropy,
The goal of which is near insanity,
When things become a bit too predictable,
And life threatens to appear all too reasonable,
The player must make a strategic move,
Or the situation will tragically improve,
One may carefully distribute loose ends randomly,
Over which to trip and stumble haphazardly,
Or ask new players to join the game,
Whose rules are inevitably not the same,
But in the face of prolonged consistency,
When control and order emerge insistently,
One must make an all-out attack,
In order to survive and bring entropy back,
There is only one thing that is a sure defense,
Against reproducibility and significance,
That's my secret and I guard it well,
And for no fortune can you make me tell,
Just watch my progress and you will see,
I will surely win the game of Entropy!

Thirty-five years later I now see the uncertainty as a gift. There are still days when I'm not sure which road to take and I'm overwhelmed by the choices unfolding in front of me. But I now know that uncertainty opens the door to possibilities.

The uncertainty we face when we leave school *never* evaporates. There is uncertainty at each turn in our lives — when we start a new job, launch a new company, begin a new relationship, have a child, or retire. Each of these decisions and actions opens the door to considerable uncertainty — and opportunity! Uncertainty is the essence of life, a fire that sparks innovation, and an engine that drives us forward.

Hopefully, the stories in this book underscore the idea that boundless possibilities result from extracting yourself from your comfort zone, being willing to fail, having a healthy disregard for the impossible, and seizing every opportunity to be fabulous. Yes, these actions inject chaos into your life and keep you off-balance. But they also take you to places you couldn't even have imagined and provide a lens through which to see problems as opportunities. Above all, they give you growing confidence that problems you face can be solved.

The poem I wrote thirty-five years ago is a poignant reminder of the uncertainty I experienced in my twenties when I looked ahead, not knowing what lay around the next curve. I wish someone had told me to embrace that uncertainty. As the stories in this book demonstrate, the most interesting things happen when you get off the predictable path, when you challenge assumptions, and when you give yourself permission to see the world as opportunity rich and full of possibility.

AUTHOR'S LETTER

Thank you so much for taking the time to read this book. I hope that the words have been meaningful to you.

It all began with the seed of an idea fourteen years ago when my son, Josh, turned sixteen. It dawned on me that he would be heading to college in only two years, and I felt remiss. Although he had learned all the traditional things we teach young people in school, I realized there were many lessons that would have made my life so much less stressful and more fulfilling when I went off to college and started my career. So, I created a growing list of things I knew were critically important in making one's place in the world. This document resided on my computer, and whenever I thought of another insight, I added it to the list.

A few months after I started my list, I was asked to give a talk to students in a business leadership program at Stanford, and I decided to use the list for inspiration. I crafted a talk called "What I Wish I Knew When I Was 20," in which I wove together these concepts with short video clips of entrepreneurial thought leaders from our Stanford lecture series. The talk resonated with the students, and soon thereafter I was asked to give this lecture in other venues, first across campus, then across the country and the world.

Buoyed by the enthusiastic response, I wrote a short book proposal on my flight back from United States Military Academy at West Point, where I had given the talk to all the new cadets. I shared the proposal with a colleague's book agent. He was not at all excited about it and suggested I go back to the drawing board. Somewhat dejected and busy with a zillion other things, I didn't revise it. The book proposal sat quietly in a file on my computer.

Two full years later, I was on an early morning flight from San Francisco, on my way to a conference in Ecuador. After breakfast was served, I started a conversation with the man sitting next to me, named Mark. He was the publisher of Harper-One in San Francisco, and by the end of the flight we had found several common interests related to education and publishing. About halfway through the flight, I took a small risk and showed him the book proposal, which was conveniently hibernating on my computer. Mark politely scanned it and told me he wasn't interested. Strike two. At the end of the flight we exchanged contact information, and I reached out to him periodically with updates on projects I was doing in my classes.

About a year after we met, I sent Mark some short videos from the Innovation Tournament, described in detail in the first chapter of this book. He was intrigued and surprisingly wanted to discuss the possibility of publishing a book with one of the student teams based on their project. Honestly, I was a bit hurt that he wanted to work on a book with my students and not with me. But, of course, I made the introductions.

Mark and his colleagues came to campus to meet with the students, who weren't interested in writing a book. They were graduating and heading off in all different directions. While on campus, I met a senior editor on Mark's team. By the end of our lunch, he suggested that I might write a book based on the work I was doing in my classes. I told him that, in fact, I already had a book proposal and sent him the exact same document I had shared with the book agent and with his boss.

Great news! Within a few weeks I had a book contract. Bad news. I had only four months in which to write the book so that it would be out in time for graduation. With six weeks of travel coming up and a full plate of other commitments, I drew upon everything I could to get this project done. I wrote three hours every morning, and anyone or anything that crossed my path during that time ended up in the book. I was a virtual vacuum for stories that reinforced the concepts. Remarkably, the book came out on Josh's twentieth birthday, and I was delighted to hand him the first copy I received.

To me, I had done my job!

But something surprising happened. The book took off, not only in the US but also around the world. The messages apparently resonated with people of all ages in vastly different cultures, including Japan, China, Korea, Thailand, Turkey, Russia, Brazil, Israel, and Germany. I started getting letters from people in these countries, saying they were hungry for the ideas in the book. Each person found different things meaningful to them. Some focused on the stories about recovering from failure, others were moved by the lessons on challenging assumptions, some were inspired by those who figured out how to leverage limited resources to accomplish remarkable things, and others were just waiting for permission to follow their own path. Hopefully, this book has provided you with fuel that will propel you into your next decade. It is remarkable what can happen in ten years!

With deep appreciation,

Tina Seelig
April 20, 2019
Portola Valley, California

ACKNOWLEDGMENTS

There are so many people to thank for helping to bring this book to life. Most important, I want to thank you. If it weren't for readers who found the original words meaningful, I would never have had a chance to create a ten-year edition of this book. I am deeply appreciative for that opportunity.

For both editions, I was fortunate to learn from the experiences of others who shared their stories and lessons with me. This includes Lisa Benatar, Soujanya Bhumkar, Steve Blank, Teresa Briggs, Peggy Burke, Tom Byers, Dana Calderwood, Stan Christensen, Sandra Cook, Michael Dearing, Ashwini Doshi, Debra Dunn, Alistair Fee, Nathan Furr, Steve Garrity, Linda Gass, Jeff Hawkins, John Hennessy, Quincy Jones III, Jeanie Kahwajy, Guy Kawasaki, Perry Klebahn, Randy Komisar, Chong Moon Lee, Fern Mandelbaum, Kevin McSpadden, Tricia Lee, Blake Nordstrom, Erik Nordstrom, Elisabeth Paté-Cornell, Jim Plummer, Bernie Roth, Heidi Roizen, Michael Rothenberg, David Rothkopf, Linda Rottenberg, Josh Schwarzepel, Jerry Seelig, Jeff Seibert, Carla Shatz, John Stiggelbout, Carlos Vignolo, Quyen Vuong, and Paul Yock.

I also want to thank all those entrepreneurial thought leaders who come to Stanford to share their experiences in our lecture series. I mined the STVP Entrepreneurship Corner (eCorner) website for lessons from the following speakers: Carol Bartz, Pat Brown, Chip Heath, Mir Imran, Leila Janah, Steve Jurvetson, David Kelley, Vinod Khosla, Marissa Mayer, Josh McFarland, David Neeleman, Larry Page, Gil Penchina, Bonny Simi, Debbie Sterling, Kevin Weil, and Anne Wojcicki. I also acknowledge Steve Jobs for his remarkable commencement address at Stanford in 2005.

My wonderful colleagues at the Stanford Technology Ventures Program (STVP) and the School of Engineering deserve considerable credit for their contributions to this project. They have all enriched my life tremendously. First, let me thank Tom Byers for inviting me to join him at STVP twenty years ago. Tom has been a terrific role model, a fabulous colleague, and a great friend. Without Tom's generous support and guidance, there is no way I would have had the opportunities that unfolded over the years.

Second, I want to call out my fantastic colleagues at STVP over the years who have taught me so much, including Ravi Balani, Steve Blank, Toby Corey, Lauren Crout, Chuck Eesley, Kathy Eisenhardt, Matt Harvey, Pam Hinds, Rebeca Hwang, Rachel Jalkowski, Riitta Katila, Harjoth Khara, Trevor Loy, Emily Ma, Fern Mandelbaum, Ann Miura-Ko, Alberto Savoia, Danielle Steussy, Forrest Glick, Theresa Lina Stevens, Alli Rico, Nikki Salgado, Ryan Shiba, Bob Sutton, and Victoria Woo; as well as my School of Engineering colleagues Nick Bambos, Margaret Brandeau, Laura Breyfogle, Jim Plummer, and Jennifer Widom, who make Stanford's School of Engineering a remarkable place to work. Special thanks go to STVP's sponsors, whose generosity allows us to educate the next generation of entrepreneurs.

I want to pay tribute to my friends and colleagues at the Hasso Plattner Institute of Design at Stanford, or d.school, over the years. Specifically, I want to call out Banny Banerjee, Michael Barry, Dennis Boyle, Bruce Boyd, Charlotte Burgess Auburn, Carissa Carter, Maureen Carroll, Rich Cox Braden, Liz Gerber, Julian Gorodsky, Justin Ferrell, Aleta Hayes, Nicole Kahn, David Kelley, George Kembel, Kim Kendall Humphreys, Hannah Joy Root, Erik Olesund, Bernie Roth, Sarah Stein Greenberg, Mark Grunberg, Alberto Savoia, Lisa Solomon, Terry Winograd, and Susie Wise, who consistently inspire me with their creativity and commitment to teaching.

It is important to acknowledge all the students with whom I have the pleasure of working, including the Mayfield Fellows, DFJ Entrepreneurial Leadership Fellows, Accel Innovation Scholars, Biodesign Fellows, the d.school Bootcamp and Summer College students, and all those in my courses on creativity and innovation. Their entrepreneurial spirit consistently exceeds all of my expectations.

There are also many people who read this manuscript in various stages of its evolution and gave me valuable feedback. This includes Ramya Balasingam, James Barlow, Sylvine Beller, Peggy Burke, Katherine Emery, Carol Eastman, Gregg Garmisa, Gerardo Gonzalez, Jonah Greenberg, Grace Isford, Boris Logvinskiy, Beata Petkowa, Patricia Ryan Madson, Juliet Rothenberg, Ali Sarilgan, Jerry Seelig, Lorraine Seelig, Anand Subramani, and Eric Volmar. Their helpful comments and suggestions had a big influence on the evolution of this book.

Even with all this support, this project would never have materialized without the guidance provided by Gideon Weil at HarperOne. He is a remarkable coach, a terrific teacher, and a wonderful editor. I learned something new in every one of our conversations over the past ten years, and always look forward to his calls. Additionally, I want to thank Lisa Zuniga for editing the first edition of the book, and Mary Grangeia and Dianna Stirpe for editing the ten-year edition. They all worked with me with great skill to make sure that the nuances of all the stories were not lost as they polished the prose.

And special thanks go to Mark Tauber for befriending me on that cross-country flight many years ago. Our story is a powerful reminder that you never know what will happen when you strike up a conversation.

On a personal note, I want to give a huge shout-out to my husband Michael, who has been an invaluable partner and advisor. I am so appreciative to Michael for his helpful suggestions, unconditional support, and unending encouragement. And special thanks go to my parents, who laid the foundation of my education. They have been wonderful role models and teachers my entire life.

Finally, I am completely indebted to Josh for inspiring me to make a list of things I wish I knew when I was twenty. Over the years he has always provided thoughtful and provocative insights on how to find one's place in the world, and I continue to be awed by his wisdom. This new edition is my thirtieth birthday present to Josh. Happy birthday . . . and many more!

NOTES

Chapter 1: Buy One, Get Two Free

1. The Hasso Plattner Institute of Design at Stanford is affectionately called the d.school. Its website is dschool.stanford.edu.
2. After reading this example in the earlier edition of this book, a few readers interpreted waiting in line for others as illegal. In fact, there are many legal businesses that provide this type of service. Examples include LineAngel (lineangel.com/) and TaskRabbit (www.taskrabbit.com/m /featured/waiting-in-line).
3. For details about the One Red Paperclip project, visit www.onered paperclip.com.
4. For Global Innovation Tournament information, visit ecorner.stanford .edu/article/how-to-run-your-own-innovation-tournament/.
5. "Imagine It Post-It Challenge," posted by Rudy Poe, April 19, 2015, video, 49:17, vimeo.com/125397870.
6. Vinod Khosla's video on turning problems into opportunities, "Any Big Problem Is a Big Opportunity," can be found at ecorner.stanford.edu /video/any-big-problem-is-a-big-opportunity.
7. The Stanford Technology Ventures Program (STVP) is hosted by the Department of Management Science and Engineering within Stanford's School of Engineering. The program's website is stvp.stanford.edu.
8. William Bruce Cameron, *Informal Sociology: A Casual Introduction to Sociological Thinking* (New York: Random House, 1963), 13.

Chapter 2: The Upside-Down Circus

1. "Do Bands," posted by BigloftRulz, February 28, 2008, video, 3:01, www.youtube.com/watch?v=gz0246tMejk.
2. Lewis Pugh, twitter.com/lewispugh/status/950579550009876480.
3. For information about Stanford's Byers Center for Biodesign program, visit biodesign.stanford.edu/.
4. This two-part case study is available through the Case Centre, www.thecasecentre.org/main/. The part titles are "The Evolution of the Circus Industry" and "Even a Clown Can Do It: Cirque du Soleil Re-creates Live Entertainment," by W. Chan Kim, Renée Mauborgne, Ben M. Bensaou, and Matt Williamson (Fontainebleau, France: INSEAD, June 2009).
5. You can find information on this lecture series at ecorner.stanford.edu /events, and all lectures are archived at ecorner.stanford.edu.
6. Alan Alda, "62nd Commencement Address," Connecticut College, June 1, 1980, digitalcommons.conncoll.edu/commence/7/.
7. Video clips of Randy Komisar can be found at ecorner.stanford.edu.
8. Video clips of Guy Kawasaki can be found at ecorner.stanford.edu.
9. "Elon Musk: How to Build the Future," interview by Jared Friedman, Y Combinator, September 15, 2016, video, 19:32, www.ycombinator.com /future/elon/.
10. Jared Lindzon, "How Sky Diving Cured My Depression," *New York Times*, April 13, 2018, www.nytimes.com/2018/04/13/opinion/depression -sky-diving-dubai.html.

Chapter 3: Bikini or Die

1. B. F. Skinner, "Selection by Consequences," *Science* 213, no. 4507 (July 31, 1981): 501–4.
2. See www.youtube.com/watch?time_continue=112&v=68JLWyPxt7g.
3. Video clips of Larry Page can be found at ecorner.stanford.edu.
4. For information about Endeavor, visit www.endeavor.org.
5. For more information, visit www.economist.com/business/2012/10/13 /shut-down-cumplo.

Chapter 4: Please Take Out Your Wallets

1. For more information about Booz Allen Hamilton, visit www.boozallen .com.
2. A video summarizing this exercise: Tina Seelig, "Wallet Prototyping," eCorner, February 6, 2007, video, 7:17, ecorner.stanford.edu/video /wallet-prototyping/.

3. Video clips of David Rothkopf can be found at ecorner.stanford.edu.
4. Video clips of Bonny Simi can be found at ecorner.stanford.edu.

Chapter 5: The Secret Sauce of Silicon Valley

1. Johannes Haushofer, "CV of Failures," www.princeton.edu/~joha
    /Johannes_Haushofer_CV_of_Failures.pdf.
2. Global Entrepreneurship Monitor: www.gemconsortium.org/.
3. Thomas Catan, "Spain's Showy Debt Collectors Wear a Tux, Collect the
    Bucks," *Wall Street Journal*, October 11, 2008, www.wsj.com/articles
    /SB122369424667425525.
4. For more about Bob Eberhart's research on Japanese laws regarding
    failure: Pui Shiau, "Changes in Regulations Boost Entrepreneurship
    in Japan," Stanford Office of International Affairs, May 21, 2012,
    international.stanford.edu/info/news/changes-regulations-boost
    -entrepreneurship-japan.
5. For more about the Mayfield Fellows Program, visit mfp.stanford.edu.
6. For more about BookScan data on book publishing rates and sales:
    Lincoln Michel, "Everything You Wanted to Know About Book Sales
    (But Were Afraid to Ask)," Electric Lit, June 30, 2016, electricliterature.
    com/everything-you-wanted-to-know-about-book-sales-but-were-afraid
    -to-ask-1fe6bc00aa2d.
7. Video clips of Mir Imran can be found at ecorner.stanford.edu.
8. Robert Sutton, *The No Asshole Rule: Building a Civilized Workplace and
    Surviving One That Isn't* (New York: Business Plus, 2010).
9. "Stanford Rubber Wishing Tree," posted by StanfordBiodesign, February
    28, 2008, video, 2:32, www.youtube.com/watch?v=YO44XJlXJjY.
10. Video clips of Gil Penchina can be found at ecorner.stanford.edu. Also
    see ecorner.stanford.edu/podcast/the-contrasts-of-a-big-company-and-a
    -small-start-up/.

Chapter 6: Turbulence Ahead

1. Video clips of Debbie Sterling can be found at ecorner.stanford.edu.
2. Alberto Savoia, *The Right It: Why So Many Ideas Fail and How to Make
    Sure Yours Succeed* (San Francisco: HarperOne, 2019).
3. Video clips of Carol Bartz can be found at ecorner.stanford.edu.
4. Josh McFarland, "Answering Common Startup Questions [Entire Talk],"
    Entrepreneurial Thought Leaders, season 13, episode 15, March 7, 2018,
    video, 59:10, ecorner.stanford.edu/video/answering-common-startup
    -questions-entire-talk/.
5. "Steve Jobs's 2005 Commencement Address," *Stanford News*, June 14,
    2005, video (and transcript), 15:04, news.stanford.edu/2005/06/14/jobs
    -061505/.

6. Video clips of David Neeleman can be found at ecorner.stanford.edu.
7. Robert Sutton, *Weird Ideas That Work* (New York: Free Press, 2002). Video clips of Bob Sutton can be found at ecorner.stanford.edu.
8. Jeff Hawkins, "Individual vs. Company," Entrepreneurial Thought Leaders, October 23, 2002, video, 1:17, ecorner.stanford.edu/video /individual-vs-company/.

Chapter 7: No Way . . . Engineering Is for Girls

1. "Mike Rowe: Don't Pursue Your Passion. Chase Opportunity," posted by Entrepreneur, April 10, 2015, video, 2:58, www.youtube.com /watch?v=NT1i26RbrhM.

Chapter 8: Turn Lemonade into Helicopters

1. For the full definition of "luck," visit en.oxforddictionaries.com /definition/luck and www.differencebetween.com/difference-between -destiny-and-vs-luck/.
2. "Princeton Baccalaureate 2012: Michael Lewis," posted by Princeton University, June 5, 2012, video, 13:41, www.youtube.com/watch?v=CiQ _T5C3hIM.
3. "Secret of Luck," posted by Nick Angel, December 23, 2011, video, 44:17, vimeo.com/34133694.
4. Tina Seelig, "The Little Risks You Can Take to Increase Your Luck," TED Talk, June 2018, video, 11:40, www.ted.com/talks/tina_seelig_the _little_risks_you_can_take_to_increase_your_luck.
5. "Steve Jobs's 2005 Commencement Address," *Stanford News*, June 14, 2005, video (and transcript), 15:04, news.stanford.edu/2005/06/14/jobs -061505/.

Chapter 9: Are You Smart or Right?

1. Robert Sutton, *The No Asshole Rule: Building a Civilized Workplace and Surviving One That Isn't* (New York: Business Plus, 2010).
2. Video clips of Guy Kawasaki can be found at ecorner.stanford.edu.
3. Greg McKeown, *Essentialism: The Disciplined Pursuit of Less* (New York: Crown, 2014).
4. A blog post on scarcity and abundance: Tina Seelig, "How to Navigate the Transition from Scarcity to Abundance," Medium, March 7, 2017, medium.com/@tseelig/when-less-is-more-navigating-the-transition -from-scarcity-to-abundance-13f3c2fc9671.

Chapter 10: Paint the Target Around the Arrow

1. This negotiation exercise is based on an exercise I observed in Maggie Neale's class at the Stanford Graduate School of Business.

2. Margaret Anne Neale, "Win More by Solving Other People's Problems," *Stanford Innovation Lab*, January 11, 2017, podcast interview, 25:56, ecorner.stanford.edu/podcast/win-more-by-solving-other-peoples -problems/.

3. Heidi Roizen, on making yourself easy to help: "Networking Expert Heidi Roizen on Making Business Connections That Matter," *Adobe Blog*, posted by Adobe Communications Team, November 1, 2017, theblog.adobe.com/heidi-roizen/.

Chapter 11: Will This Be on the Exam?

1. Video clips of Steve Garrity can be found at ecorner.stanford.edu.

2. Video clips of Kevin Weil can be found at ecorner.stanford.edu.

3. Chip Heath, "A Well-Designed First Day," Entrepreneurial Thought Leaders, May 7, 2018, video, 4:24, ecorner.stanford.edu/in-brief/a-well -designed-first-day/.

4. A short video summarizing the puzzle exercise: Tina Seelig, "The Puzzle Project: Entrepreneurship Simulation," eCorner, September 21, 2006, video, 5:45, ecorner.stanford.edu/video/the-puzzle-project -entrepreneurship-simulation/.

Chapter 12: Experimental Artifacts

1. For more information, visit www.embraceinnovations.com/#home; also visit ecorner.stanford.edu/video/embrace-the-entrepreneurial-journey/.

2. Video clips of David Kelley can be found at ecorner.stanford.edu.

3. For more information about this program, visit chipconley.com/modern -elder-academy.

4. For more information, visit www.positiveintelligence.com/assessments/.

INDEX

23andMe, 28–29

A-B testing, 91–92
Adams, Jim, 142–43
Airbnb, 48
Alda, Alan, 31
Antarctica, 43
Apple Computer, 77, 87–88
Apple Newton, 18
appreciation, 20, 24, 84, 137–39
Art of Innovation, The (Kelley), 46
assumptions, 26–31, 36, 48, 52,
    155, 180
automatic teller machines (ATMs), 24

baby incubator, 180–82
balloon angioplasty, 23, 27
banking regulations, 39
bankruptcy laws, 72–73
Barlow, James, 32
Barry, Michael, 24–25
Bartz, Carol, 86
being fabulous, 163–68, 171, 177
Beleza Natural, 38
best alternative to a negotiated
    agreement (BATNA), 158
best ideas exercise, 41, 43
bikinis, 43

Biodesign Fellows, 22–23
Bio-X, 56
BookBrowser, 54
book publishing industry, 54–55,
    75–76
BookScan, 75
Booz Allen Hamilton (Booz Allen), 57
Braden, Rich, 27
bra-fitting service, 33
brainstorming, 33, 45–47
Briggs, Teresa, 108–9
Brown, Pat, 29
Burbn, 17
Burke, Peggy, 189–90
Byers, Tom, 74

Calderwood, Dana, 133–35
car purchase, 155–56
Carter, Jimmy, 63
cell phones, 24
challenging assumptions exercise,
    30–31
Chamine, Shirzad, 186–87
Children's Discovery Museum of San
    Jose, 102
Chile, 38–40
Christensen, Stan, 157–58
Circus, At the (Marx Brothers), 26

circus exercise, 26–27
Cirque du Soleil, 26–27
Claris, 77–78
college admissions application, 43–45
competition, 172–75
Conley, Chip, 184
construction toys, 83–84
Crazy Is a Compliment (Rottenberg), 38
creative writing class assignment, 182–84
Cumplo, 38–39
customer satisfaction, 175–77

DARPA Grand Challenge, 95
"da Vinci Rule, The," 76
Dearing, Michael, 58–59
decision-making, 94–95, 105
Defense Advanced Research Projects Agency (DARPA), 95
Deloitte, 108–9
diaper sales, 25
Dirty Jobs (television show), 100
dishwashing, 28
Do Bands bracelets, 20
Doshi, Ashwini, 164–166
Dweck, Carol, 65

Eberhart, Bob, 73
education, 10–12
Einstein, Albert, 22
Embrace (baby incubator), 180–82
Empire Strikes Back, The (film), 169
Endeavor, 37, 49, 180
Entrepreneurial Thought Leaders series, 29
entrepreneurship, 7–8, 32–33, 57, 74–75, 172–75
"Entropy" (Seelig), 193
excuses, 169
expectations, 51–52, 164, 166–68
Experimental Artifacts (Seelig), 193

failure, 12, 69–80, 87–91
failure résumé assignment, 69–72
family obligations, 110–12
fear, 32, 33–34
fifty British pounds challenge, 32–33
Five-Dollar Challenge, 1–8, 31
Furr, Nathan, 100–101

Garrity, Steve, 167
Garten, Jeffrey, 63–64
genetic testing, 28–29
Glick, Forrest, 161
Global Entrepreneurship Monitor (GEM), 72
GoldieBlox, 83
Google, 36, 91
gratitude, 137
Greatest Show on Earth, 27

Haig, Alexander, 63
hair product, 38
Handspring, 18
Haushofer, Johannes, 72
Hawkins, Jeff, 17–19, 96
Heath, Chip, 170
Heath, Dan, 170
housekeeping, 28
Huggies diapers, 24–25
HyperCard, 54

idea generation, 41–48, 57–58, 129–35
IDEO design firm, 46
Imagine It! (documentary film), 7
Impossible Foods, 29
Improv Wisdom (Madson), 46
Imran, Mir, 76
Innovation Tournament, 15, 20, 22, 77, 196
Institut Européen d'Administration des Affaires (INSEAD), 100

International Media Partners, 62–63
iPod Nano, 163

Janah, Leila, 29
Japan, 73
JetBlue, 89
jigsaw puzzles exercise, 172–74
Jobs, Steve, 87–90, 128–29
John Deere (tractor manufacturer), 170–71
Jones, Quincy, III, 114–16

Kahwajy, Jeannie, 143–44
Kawasaki, Guy, 31, 144–45
Kelley, David, 46, 182
Kelley, Tom, 46
Kimberly-Clark, 24–25
Kisenwether, Liz, 69
Kissinger, Henry, 62–64
Kissinger Associates, Inc., 64
Klebahn, Perry, 98, 131–33
Komisar, Randy, 31, 73, 77–78, 146
Krieger, Mike, 17

Laliberté, Guy, 26
Lao-tzu, 99
leadership roles, 53, 61–62
Lewis, Michael, 116–17
Liar's Poker (Lewis), 116–17
Lindzon, Jared, 33–34
lottery, 64
luck, 113–29, 135, 144
Lyft, 48

MacDonald, Kyle, 5
Macintosh, 87
Madson, Patricia Ryan, 46
Mandelbaum, Fern, 150–51
Marshall, Morgan, 28
Marx Brothers, 26
Mayfield Fellows Program, 74–75
McFarland, Josh, 86–87

McKeown, Greg, 148
medical devices, 55–56, 105
Modern Elder Academy, 184–85
Monk and the Riddle, The (Komisar), 31
Morris Air, 89
Moto Restaurant, 50
Musk, Elon, 32
My Dinner with Andre (movie), 36

Neale, Maggie, 155
"need finding," 22–25
Neeleman, David, 88
negotiations, 81, 154–59
Netflix, 48
new employees, 170–71
New York Times, 33
NeXT, 88
No Asshole Rule, The (Sutton), 76
Nordstrom, Blake, 175–77
Nordstrom, Erik, 175–77
Nordstrom Inc., 175–77
Noyce, Bob, 87
Numenta, 19

O'Connor, Sandra Day, 111
Olympic Games, 66–67
On Intelligence (Hawkins), 19
opportunity cost, 137–38
Or, Tyranny of the, 150

Packard, David, 87
Page, Larry, 36
"Paint the target around the arrow," 161
Palm Computing, 17–18
Pampers, 25
paper clips exercise, 5–6, 31
Parsons, Estelle, 134
Pasteur, Louis, 117
Paté-Cornell, Elisabeth, 94
peer-to-peer lending platform, 38–39

Penchina, Gil, 80
photo service, 58
Pixar, 87–88
Plummer, Jim, 91
political parties platform, 39–40
Post-it notes exercise, 6–7
Powell Jobs, Laurene, 88
Power of Moments, The (Heath and Heath), 170
preconceptions, 102–4
"pretotyping," 85
Princeton University, 72, 116–17
"problem blindness," 24
Procter & Gamble, 25
product design, 22, 59–61
Professional Happiness Design (PHD) exercise, 65–67
Pugh, Lewis, 21
Pull-Ups, 25

quitting, 76–77, 81–83

RCA Corporation, 191
Reagan, Ronald W., 63
recommendation letter, 44–45, 157
Red Hot Chili Peppers, 159
Right It, The (Savoia), 85
right thing, 146–48
Ringling Bros. and Barnum & Bailey Circus, 26–27
risk management, 94
Risk-o-Meter, 92–94
risks, 29, 65–67, 72–73, 91–94
Roche, Ben, 50
Roizen, Heidi, 161
Roth, Bernie, 168–69
Rothkopf, David, 61–64
Rothkopf Group, The, 62
Rottenberg, Linda, 37, 49
Rowe, Mike, 100
rubber bands exercise, 78–79

Rubesch, Ed, 156
rule breaking, 48–52
rules/norms, 35–36, 48–52

Salomon Brothers, 116–17
Samasource, 29
"Sand" (Seelig), 185
Savoia, Alberto, 85
Scientific American, 54
"Secret of Luck, The" (video), 125
self-assessment, 109–10
Shea, Nicolas, 38–40
shoeshine stand, 33
Silicon Valley, 73
Simi, Bonny, 66–67
Simpson, John, 23
Skinner, B. F., 35
Slack, 17
smart thing, 146–48
snowshoes, 98, 131–33
social rules/norms, 35–36
Southwest Airlines, 89
SpaceX, 48
Spain, 73
speed-dating station, 33
Stanford Magazine, 111
Stanford University
    Artificial Intelligence Laboratory, 95
    Biodesign program, 22, 55
    commencement address, 87–88, 128–29
    Design for Extreme Affordability class, 180
    d.school, 9–10, 59, 61, 91, 168, 181–82
    Entrepreneurial Thought Leaders lecture series, 170
    medical device testing, 105
    psychology department, 65
    School of Engineering, 8, 91, 125
    Stanford Sierra Camp, 28

Stanford Technology Ventures
    Program, 8–10, 29
"Stanley," 95–96
Start-Up Chile, 38–39
Sterling, Debbie, 83
Stiggelbout, John, 43–45
Superclass (Rothkopf), 62
Sutton, Bob, 76–77, 90
Sweden, 72–73
Systrom, Kevin, 17

team players, 160–61, 172–74
Tech Museum of Innovation,
    The, 142
Thailand, 72
to-do list, 149
Todos ("everyone"), 39–40
Toy Story (film), 88

"umbrella walkers," 32–33
uncertainty, 108, 193–94
University of California at Santa
    Cruz, 104–5

value, 5–6, 31
vegetarian meat substitute, 29
Velez, Leila, 37–38
Vignolo, Carlos, 11
Visor, 18–19
Volkswagen Electronics Research
    Laboratory, 95

wallet exercise, 59–61
Wall Street Journal, 73, 145
water bottle exercise, 168
Web of Secrets, 79
Weil, Kevin, 168
Weird Ideas That Work (Sutton), 90
Wiseman, Richard, 123, 133
Wishing Tree, 78–79
Wojcicki, Anne, 28–29
World Economic Forum, 62
worst ideas exercise, 41–43

Yock, Paul, 22–23, 55–56

Zoomer, 18